REALITY

What a Wild Ride!

Text Copyright © 2008 by Travis Hatch

Permission for 'The Canoe Trip' and 'My Christmas Poem' kindly given by Kyla Hatch

Illustration Copyright © 2008 by Levi Hatch

National Library of Canada Cataloguing in Publication Data

Hatch, Travis-
Reality: What a Wild Ride!

ISBN 978-0-9809831-0-4

Published by Brenda Giesbrecht,
'A Way With Words', 2008

All rights reserved. No part of this publication may be reproduced, stored in a retrieval system or transmitted in any form or by any means - electronic, mechanical, photocopying, recording or otherwise - without prior written permission of the author.

Printed and Bound in Canada by
Blitzprint, Calgary, Alberta
www.blitzprint.com

It's an odd job, making people laugh.
— Moliere

Contents

Disclaimer 6
Livestock Transport 7
Black Ford Truck 13
Laughin' 23
Friends 24
The Battle 34
Grade Three 36
The Chocolate Milk Machine 40
Team Drivers 42
Cowboy's Dream 46
Helping Dad 47
Betsy and the Bar 51
Revenge 52
Uncle Joe 59
Frogs 60
Cowboy Poetry 62
How to Wear Out a Washing Machine .. 64
Alfred's Truck 69
Bender and Brown 71
Chewin' Gum 72
Crushed 73
Living in the Cemetery 80
Telephoning 86
The Hero 88
Blank Pages 92
The Canoe Trip 93
Oh Christmas Tree 97
Milking the Dragon 98
Brown Christmas 105
The Swimming Hole 106
Me and Mine Bruther Jake 109
The Baptism 110
One More as He Goes 113
The Bus 114

Family Tree	124
Snake Hill	126
The Aristocrat	128
The Hazards of Friendships	129
Tractor Song	142
Bears	143
No Longer Welcome	151
Aunt Inez	152
Sugar and Cream	157
Habits	158
Survival of the Fittest	159
Lost Horse Treasure	160
Whoa Mule, Whoa!	162
Raising my Siblings	163
When You're Feeling Important	166
Emerson's Turnip Recipe	167
Old Grimes is Dead	170
Just Give 'er. It'll Heal	171
Hatch's Rendition of "Last Kiss...mas"	179
No Talent	180
Wipe Out	182
UFA Meeting	184
The Wheel	187
The Chefs	193
The Dump	195
The Dump Song	196
Hair Cut	198
The Moskeeter	201
My Christmas Poem	202
The Helper	204
A Man's Life	206
Little Girls	208
Hayden	209
The Little House	217

*D*isclaimer

In northeastern Alberta there is a small community called Cherry Grove which was settled at the beginning of the Great Depression. The land is rocky and rough and won't grow much except poplar trees and willows. As a result, the depression in that area lasted well into the 1960s. One of the families that settled the area was the family of Victor and Susan Hatch, my great grandparents. They came in 1932 and stayed because they didn't have enough money to leave. Most of their twelve children raised their families there. My grandfather raised his eleven children and they, in turn, stayed and had children of their own. I was quite old before I realized that there were people in the world who weren't my cousins.

Such large families also created a situation where my Aunts Marian and Kay and my Uncles Jim and Ed are closer in age to me than my own brothers and sister. I spent much of my childhood with them and they virtually became my siblings and treated me just as badly as if I was.

Someone once said that the only difference between fiction and non-fiction is that fiction has to make some sort of sense. This compilation of stories is my life history and is non-fiction, and I make no apologies. It may not be in chronological order but that won't be surprising to those who know me. I never lived my life chronologically either. I was an old man when I was twelve years old and started my carefree youth when I turned 36. I married Helen in 1986 and then, after awhile, we fell in love. A couple of years ago we began dating and we are currently planning our honeymoon. So it shouldn't surprise anybody that the rest of my life wasn't any different.

Every story I tell here is exactly the way I remember it. If there is any discrepancy between reality and my memory, I'll swear by the memory. I have found that reality can't always be trusted. Reality has always had a warped view of me and has let me down on many occasions. I don't trust it.

So as you read, you can rest assured that it happened just the way I tell it. If your memory of the following events is different, it's because your memory isn't as accurate as mine. I have 98% total recall. No, wait a minute. I think it might have been 96%. Either way, I can remember almost everything I have ever done or heard in my life, including the things I saw and heard my uncles and aunts do. So if they don't ante up and buy multiple copies of this book to give to their children and grandchildren I will write volume two entitled "What Your Parents Were Really Like" and I'll sell it to their kids one page at a time. You may think that this is extortion. You are right.

My sister Shelby graduated from nursing school and applied for a job in a psychiatric ward. The interviewer asked if she had any experience and she said yes, she had been raised in an undiagnosed psych ward. She got the job. Such is my family. I am the only sane one of the bunch, which is why they call me the white sheep of the family.

None of the names have been changed to protect anybody, because none of the people mentioned are innocent.

There are a few stories and poems that are included just for fun.

A few of the recitations and songs are from my Great Grandfather Victor Hatch. He had the reputation of being somewhat of a comedian or what would be known today as a Cowboy Poet.

I recall as a youth, sitting with my many cousins as we listened to him recite and sing goofy songs. He had seemingly countless songs and recitations in his head and could recite non-stop for an hour without repetition.

He currently has descendants that number in the thousands. As far as I know I am the only one who remembers his songs and recitations. Many of my relatives remember listening to him, and have their favorite song or recitation that I have been requested to perform at family reunions. I have included the recitations I have in my possession in this book to give my many cousins an opportunity to share that part of our heritage with their own children. I do not know the original source of all his material but I'm sure most of it came out of his own fertile mind. His pieces are identified with a covered wagon logo on the page, in commemoration of his trek from Glenwood to Cherry Grove in 1932.

I sincerely hope that this collection sparks some of your own memories that you will share with your children and I hope it brings a smile to your day.

Livestock Transport

Jim owned a maroon colored Chevy Chevelle. It was a two door coupe, kind of a sporty looking sedan, not a true sports car but close enough that we thought it looked cool. And better yet, we thought we looked cool when we were in it. It sat so low to the ground that when Jim was chasing sheep across the pasture, the smallest rock would rip the tail pipe off. Jim was always dragging the muffler off, or it could be that he would never put it back on. Either way it sounded cool, just like a dragster or maybe a 44 Massey tractor.

This was Jim's babe-mobile. Jim and I would go to the drive-in and cruise Main Street looking and sounding real cool, secure in the knowledge that all the babes who saw us wished they could have a ride in the babe-mobile.

One day Jim phoned and announced that he was going to the auction sale in Bonnyville to see if he could buy a bum lamb or calf to put on one of his milk cows, and he invited me along. We were headed for Bonnyville, which was certainly a good place to try out the babe-mobile. Nobody knew us there.

I asked Jim how he planned to get any livestock home after he bought them. He told me that would be no problem. One small calf would fit in the back seat without any trouble. So away we went.

Things went really well at the auction, in fact prices were so good Jim wound up buying ten chickens, five ducks and a calf. I never said a word, for you see I have always had a lot of faith in Jim's ability to deal with animal crises. Ever since I've known him he's been in the middle of an animal-related problem so he's very experienced. He said it's a simple matter of throwing the birds in a bag. We borrowed a gunny sack from the auction and stuffed all the birds in the bag. The calf went into the back seat along with the bag. We piled in and headed for home.

"We just have to stop for some gas," said Jim, "then we're headed home." As we headed to downtown Bonnyville for gas we noticed that things were really quiet in the back. Jim asked me to check the bag.

"With fifteen birds in the bag, maybe they are suffocating. Open the bag," said Jim "so they can breathe a little."

I turned around to the back seat and untied the string on the bag. As the light entered the bag every bird thought it could see an escape route and they all came boiling out like the bag was on fire.

Birds are kind of like flies. They can't learn that glass is impenetrable. The chickens began flapping around the interior of the car at supersonic speed, or at least their best possible attempt at it, each one in a different orbit, bouncing off the glass as they tried to escape and squawking for all they were worth, very much like a squadron of kamikaze dive bombers on crack cocaine, complete with small but potent bombs, which they jettisoned on each pass. The calf thought this was an air assault upon him personally and tried every escape route he thought possible, trying to climb into the front seat, bellowing for his mother with all the volume he could muster.

As Jim pulled up to a gas station he commented that it was good we were at a full serve station rather than self serve or we might lose some of our birds if we tried to get the door open. The gas station attendant came out to the car but stopped a few yards away with a puzzled look on his face. Jim rolled his window down about two inches. Three birds spotted the gap and thought if they could take a run at the new opening they might make it. All three got their heads out and began to squawk and quack as if they were calling the pump jockey to come rescue them.

Jim shouted, "Twenty dollars worth, please!"

The pump jockey started as if surprised to hear human voices in the middle of the cacophony and jumped to fill the car. Jim slipped a twenty dollar bill through the crack in the window to the young man, and he stood looking after us as we sped off.

The calf, meanwhile, thinking that if he unloaded some excess weight he could jump higher or bawl louder, unloaded all he had in him on the back seat. Each bird, as it made its orbit, would bounce off the seat using it as a springboard to gain greater velocity for their next assault on the windshield and in so doing, became feathered sponges with the result that the calf's contribution was almost instantly deposited as a thin film over the entire interior of the car glass. Jim had to lean forward and squint to see through the brownish green tint on the windows. He tromped on the accelerator in a desperate attempt to get home before something bad happened.

The stench of bird manure, feathers and calf manure was beginning to make my eyes burn. I rolled down my window just enough that I could stick my lips and nose out the crack. In order to keep my nose and lips out the crack, I had to kneel up on the seat and push my face into the small gap in the window. In this position I felt safe from further buffeting in the face by the feathered dive bombers.

Things were getting desperate, though. With the chickens and ducks crying foul, the calf bawling and no muffler, we could hardly hear the radio. To top it off Jim was driving way over the speed limit, the poor engine roaring for all it was worth.

I held my breath and turned to look. The calf was trying to get back into the back seat and had one hoof down the back of Jim's shirt. Jim looked like a man possessed. His face was red and flushed like his allergies were in high gear. His eyes were bloodshot and streaming, but no wonder – he wasn't blinking. He was leaned over the steering wheel, steering with one hand, the other alternately wiping the tinting off the windshield and deflecting chickens away from his line of sight. Sweat was steaming down his face and dripping off the end of his nose onto the feathers that were stuck in his beard. His mouth was wide open but because of the noise I couldn't tell if he was just trying to breath or if he was screaming or yelling something.

At that moment an RCMP patrol car pulled up along side of us with his lights flashing, motioning for us to pull over. Jim did not even see him. The officer gazed at Jim for a moment, then turned his lights off, slowed down and stopped and was still sitting in the middle of the road as we went over the hill.

I had to breathe again so I stuck my face back into the crack. We passed numerous cars in our mad fight for survival, but in my awkward position I could not see if they noticed anything odd or not. Survival was our paramount occupation for the next twenty five minutes.

We slid to a stop in a cloud of dust in front of Jim's mobile home. "Where are we going to put these chickens, Jim?" I shouted.

"Take them into the house," he replied. "We'll put them in the back bedroom with the other ones."

The next time the babe-mobile had an outing, we wore lots of cologne and were lucky enough not to have dates.

My cousin Bryce showed me how to pick up cute girls one day. We went to the roller rink and he demonstrated his technique. He put on his roller skates and pointed out to me which girl he was going to ask out. He then skated out in front of her and fell down, flopping on the ground and flailing his arms around. The girl couldn't avoid his out stretched hand and ran over his fingers with her roller skates. She felt terrible about it so he asked her out and she said yes.

He told me it worked every time, but he only tried it once at the ice rink.

*B*lack *F*ord *T*ruck

*M*y Uncle Gary asked me if I could fix his truck. He thought it might have carburetor problems. I told him that of course I could fix it. I was fifteen years old and had taken an industrial arts class in grade 10 so I knew pretty well all there was to know about mechanics and engineering.

It was a '67 Ford half ton, painted black with a spray can to disguise the rust. It had a three speed transmission with the gear lever on the steering column. When I went to drive it home to work on it, I discovered that it had a whole lot more than carburetor problems.

It had one partial brake on the passenger side rear wheel. I discovered that as I went though the stop sign at the bottom of the hill. When I turned the wheel hard to the left to avoid the dead end sign, the transmission shifted out of third into neutral and the gas pedal stuck to the floor. I made the turn with my left foot on the clutch while trying to hook my right foot under the brake pedal so I could lift it back up for another try. When I straightened the wheel out, the transmission shifted back into third. The throttle was still on the floor and the motor at about 5000 rpm, so I let out the clutch.

Before I reached the next hard turn I'd learned that I could shift gears simply by turning the steering wheel. It seems the mounting brackets that held the cab to the frame had rusted through, and the cab had fallen two inches so that it was resting on the frame. This also caused the steering linkage and the steering column to bind up because of the weight of the front of the cab resting on it. If I jerked it hard to the right and then left again I could get the cab to rock up off the frame on one side and the throttle linkage would come unstuck, too. So it was a relatively simple matter of throwing the truck into an almost out of control sideways skid on the gravel to get the cab airborne long enough to get it throttled down and out of gear. Slowing down or stopping was accomplished by pumping the brake pedal.

This entailed tromping on it, then hooking my toe under the pedal, lifting it back up then tromping on it again. With only a half mile of this frantic exercise I made the next turn with all four wheels on the ground.

The repair of this steering and shifting problem was very simple – I just took Dad's cutting torch and blew a hole through the firewall around the steering column. When the final cut was made, the cab fell another inch so that the floorboards of the cab rested directly on the frame. This hole in the firewall around the steering column, surprisingly, not only stopped the shift linkage and throttle linkage from binding, but it also made it unnecessary to replace the heat gauge, because the fan would blow the smoke and steam directly onto my left knee whenever it overheated, negating the need for a heat gauge.

I did a minor tune-up on it by replacing a missing sparkplug cable and installing a fuel filter. I then tied what was left of the exhaust pipe up to the frame with some barbed wire and threw the muffler into the bush. It wasn't connected to the exhaust anyway and besides, there was a mouse nest in it.

Dad hadn't driven his Jeep for a long time so I pulled a couple of good tires off of it and put them on the truck. Lastly, I took a crimping tool and pinched off the three bad brake lines that had leaked out all the brake fluid, and there it was, all fixed up and road worthy again.

I gave my uncle a repair bill for $50.00, for the two wheels off the Jeep and my labour. He told me I was trying to cheat him by billing him for more than the value of the truck and said he wasn't going to pay such an outrageous bill. I told him I couldn't charge less because, technically, they were Dad's tires. Faced with the prospects of driving the truck, he came to his senses, signed the back of the registration card and the truck was mine. Looking back now I think I gave him too good of a deal. I should have asked for the fifty bucks, too - he probably would have paid it.

But I was fifteen years old and figured I had the world by the tail. I had my own truck.

My friends were all jealous and very impressed by my good fortune. I took Darrell out for a drive. We were now men of the world. We pulled out onto the open road (actually it was the back road down to the gravel pit) and we let her go. With my left elbow leaning out the window and my shades on, I looked just as cool as if I was driving a Porsche and I was just as happy as if I was in my right mind.

We opened 'er up to see what she could do. We ran out of nerve at 50 mph. The wind rocked the cab up off the frame and as it rocked back and forth it kind of threw off my steering a little because the cab would shift direction but the wheels didn't and when I steered to correct the perceived problem the cab would shift the other way and the truck would head for the trees.

I quickly learned how to compensate for the error in perception and away we went.

Darrell said, "Looks like the hood is open."

"Nah," I replied. "It always looks like that."

I was wrong. It popped open and slammed into the windshield. The hood never even slowed down. The hinges ripped right out of the rusty fenders and the hood flipped up and over the cab and landed in the box. There was no use in slowing down then, so I kept the pedal to the metal.

I looked over at Darrell and he was white as a sheet. "How do you like it?" I asked.

"I've never seen anything like it," he replied through clenched teeth.

I offered to drive him home but he told me he was training for the provincial cross country track meet and the ten mile run home would do him good, so I let him out and he started running for home.

Having such a vehicle naturally brought with it fame and prestige. I would stop for the mail at the general store and Helen, who ran the post office, would have my mail sitting on the counter.

"I heard you coming," she would say "and I got your mail ready so you wouldn't have to stay too long."

When you're well liked, you get good service.

Darrell's dad told his kids that they were not allowed to ever, under any circumstance, get in that truck. I assume it was because he was afraid his boys would want one just like it. They were not as affluent as we were and he wouldn't be able to afford it.

Buster was a mouse who lived somewhere in the truck. I believe he came from the family who used to live in the muffler, but he bore me no malice for evicting his relatives. He was quite shy at first and would only peek out at me once in awhile. Once he saw that I was not going to eat him the first chance I had, he became braver and would venture out into full view and go about his business as if I didn't exist. After a month or so, Buster would be climbing up onto the back of the seat whenever we traveled, and he would gaze out at the scenery. He never let me touch him but I considered him my pet and would tell him all the secrets of my life. One evening I sat at the beach at French Bay and talked to him for several hours. He just sat and looked at me with those sympathetic, beady little eyes as if to say, "Ya, whatever."

One day I left a bag of sunflower seeds open on the seat. When I got back in a couple days later I reached into the bag, grabbed a handful full of spits and shoved them all in my mouth. They were all opened shells with no seeds left. There were only a couple of shrivelled brown ones but they didn't taste very good. So I took another mouthful, same thing, no seeds, just empty shells. I realized Buster had been into my bag of spits. I had to go through three or four handfuls to get down to one he hadn't stolen the seeds out of. The whole rest of the bag had those little black seeds that I would have to spit out whenever I tasted one.

One frosty morning I turned on the heater fan and discovered where he had set up housekeeping. Bits of the seat cushion foam came out of the defrost vents, along with a grinding noise from the fan. I never saw him again.

Prior to that fateful day he had always shown great curiosity in what I was doing and where we were going, but after that I was left with very few friends who would ride in my truck. I have never met another mouse that I liked better, but he sure stunk up the cab for the next month whenever it got warm.

The door hinges had rusted away where they were attached to the cab, which allowed the driver's door to hang down a little in the front. This fact, combined with the fact that the weather stripping was gone, created a gap between the cab and door big enough to stick your finger through. I soon discovered that if I took some burlap sacks and rags and jammed them into the crack with a screwdriver, it kept the dust out and eliminated at least one rattle.

The starter solenoid was shot, so being the inventive mechanic that I was, I ran two heavy wires from the starter into the cab through the glove box. When the glove box was closed there was four inches of each wire hanging out very conveniently. Each wire had one inch of plastic removed, exposing the copper wire beneath. So all one had to do was turn on the key, then touch the two bared wires together. This would effectively short out the solenoid and start the engine. I didn't need anything as complicated as a working solenoid. Besides, a new one would have cost money and would have reduced my financial resources to the point where I would have been unable to go to the drive-in with my girlfriend (if I had a girlfriend, one must keep one's options open).

    My cousin Kelly and I stopped at the A&W one day. It was one of those old fashioned drive-in restaurants where you drove up in front of a long awning and turned your lights on when you were ready to order. The beautiful, young, prospective date would then come and take your order, then bring it out to you and hang the little tray from your window, thus allowing you at least two opportunities to ask her out.

    Kelly and I sat for fifteen minutes trying frantically to get her attention. Every time she would look our way we would wave and gesture and try to get her to come over to the truck. Finally when we were just about convinced that she was deliberately ignoring us for some reason, she came out and walked over toward our truck. She was better looking than we had first thought. This was going to take a very smooth and polished display of charm to impress her, but we were up to the challenge.

    She slowly walked toward the truck with a look of trepidation on her face and came around to my side of the truck. I took off my cool shades and laid them on the dash, acting very suave and debonair and began to roll down the side window. The glass fell off the front of the track inside the door and wedged itself at a forty five degree angle against the winding linkage inside. It would not roll up or down. I glanced at the waitress. She was still standing there waiting, chewing a big wad of gum and acting as though we were some species of pond scum in which she had no interest at all.

    I wrestled with the knob. With a snap it came off in my hand and I chucked it on the floor. I was getting frantic. I was going to miss my chance to ask her out if she gave up and left. I grabbed the door latch to open the door and threw my shoulder against it but the rags had it jammed too tightly. She started to back up a little with one eyebrow raised as I began ripping the rags and sacks out of the crack in the door. I tried the latch again and hit the door again with my shoulder. With a screech and bang it flung open and the window fell down completely inside the door. I looked up at the waitress and there she was, gone. I jumped out of the truck and looked around thinking that the door had knocked her down when it popped open.

    She was standing on Kelly's side of the truck. He rolled down his window.

    "Can't you boys read?" she asked, as if we looked like a couple of hicks. "You're supposed to turn on your lights when you are ready to order."

Kelly didn't appear to be listening because he was slouched down in his seat with his head down but he mumbled, "We know. We don't have any lights."

"Do you have money?"

I could have sworn she asked it with a sneer in her voice but it could have been the gum in her cheek. Kelly placed our order and she left.

"Are you going to ask her out?" I queried.

"Are you kidding?" Kelly shot back. "What if I got to know her and she figured out that I was related to you?"

I didn't see how that would make any difference but I let it lay.

When she came back, I was surprised to see she went directly to Kelly's window and deposited the tray with our burgers on it. When we were finished eating I was still hoping for one more chance to impress the girl. She came to collect the tray and then just stood there with the tray, looking at us as if she was expecting something interesting to happen.

"Let's go!" Kelly hissed under his breath, "Let's get out of here!"

"Well, start the truck then," I said.

He grabbed the two wires and touched them together. There were the usual sparks and smoke and the motor turned over but it wouldn't start. The wires were getting hot and the plastic coating burst into flames, sticking to Kelly's fingers. He yelled something that I didn't catch and beat his fingers on the dash board to put out the flames.

I began screaming at him, "Pull the wires apart before you fry my starter!!"

He made another grab for the wires and made a heroic effort to pull them apart but they had welded themselves together. The starter was still cranking the motor over. I jumped over to Kelly's side of the truck making a frantic grab for the wires and managed to get them apart. The engine quit turning over and I fell back against the seat sitting in the middle of the truck right up against Kelly. We both sat there for a minute as the smoke cleared and he gave me an elbow in the ribs to hint that maybe I should slide back over to my side of the truck.

"Why didn't it start?" Kelly seemed a little agitated at that point and began sucking on his blistered fingers

The waitress was still standing there beside Kelly's door and she did seem to be a little more interested in us than she had been before.

"Try it again, Kelly," I whispered, "This time I'll turn the key on."

His first blow caught me on the ear but the second I deflected with my elbow.

"You idiot!" he screamed, "You have the IQ of a toad stool!"

He wasn't going to get a date with that display of temper but I didn't point it out to him. He looked at the waitress and then, putting on a brave show, touched the two wires together again. There was the smoke and sparks but this time the truck started with a roar and a cloud of blue smoke poured out from underneath the cab. The waitress took a step back.

When I had cut the firewall out, the shift linkage had changed some how so that it took two people to shift it into reverse. One person jerked on the lever and the other person tried to rock the cab back and forth to get the tension out of the linkage so that it would have enough movement to shift into gear. Now, at the critical moment, Kelly wouldn't put his heart into rocking the cab.

"Harder, Kelly! Try jumping up and down more."

But his heart wasn't in it.

"Okay, I have an idea. If you jump up at the same time that I am jumping down it will rock more."

Getting the timing just right was very difficult, it seemed as though we would either jump up together or down together. I kept hitting my head on the roof of the cab, and with two guys jumping up and down in the confines of a truck cab, I could see that we weren't gaining either on the shifting or in our efforts to impress the waitress or the other people who had gathered to watch.

"Let's just push it!!" he bellowed, getting out of the truck.

Poor Kelly seemed to be getting even testier, but to humour him, I got out. The waitress took a step back with a distinct look of fear in her eyes, but when she saw we were tying to push the truck back she showed a little more interest again. I noticed that several more people had gathered to watch. It was then that I figured out what was bothering Kelly. He didn't like having an audience when he's trying to put the moves on a pretty young waitress.

There was too much of an incline and we couldn't get the truck back more than a few feet, so we got back in and tried reverse again. But Kelly wasn't helping at all now so there was no use in me jumping up and down by myself. I had no choice but to put it into first gear and drive over the parking curb, under the awning and over the curb on the other side and out onto the road.

Kelly didn't talk to me all the way home. I could tell he was upset about something, probably the fact that he had forgotten to ask her out.

My mother rode in the truck only once. Buster had passed away the fall before and was dried up enough that I couldn't smell him anymore. It was spring again. The blob of frozen turkey manure that had served as a hood ornament all winter had softened and slid off, leaving a white pinstripe effect, diagonally across the hood and off on the passengers side fender. I had placed a blanket over the seat where the upholstery had caught fire, and with these improvements made I was able to convince my mother to ride home from church with me one warm afternoon. My sister Shelby told Mum that she would come along, too, to give Mum some moral support. After church I went out to the parking lot and inspected the tie rod I had welded back on and waited for Mum to come out of the church.

The sun was shining, the snow was melting and water was running everywhere. It was such a wonderful day I hardly noticed that Mum wouldn't come out of the church until everyone else had left.

Mum and my sister crawled into the truck, trying their best to keep their Sunday dresses from getting snagged on the seat springs or muddy from the layer of goo that was caked on the outside of the truck.

Mum knew about my starting procedure but wouldn't help, so I touched the two bare wires together myself and we were off.

We had a beautiful, uneventful drive home. As I turned into the driveway I turned and asked them, "See? That wasn't so bad, was it?"

Mum looked straight and said, "We're not home yet."

Our drive way was half a mile long and had two creeks that ran across it in the spring. By mid-spring the run off and the passing vehicles had churned those two spots into mudbog supertracks.

They were so bad that sometimes we had to leave a vehicle at the main road and walk the half mile out even if we had four wheel drive.

That was Dad's idea, though. I thought if he would just get it up into high gear he could go right through, no problem. But you know old men. He was almost 38 years old and ready to turn into a fossil any day.

I told Mum, "Don't worry, we can drive all the way and you won't have to walk at all."

Mum tried to be polite and said she would prefer to walk, but I wouldn't hear of it. My mother was 38 years old, too, and I wasn't going to let a feeble old woman be forced to walk and get her shoes dirty.

The first hole was the worst. It was about fifty yards across and Dad's 4x4 had just been through dragging bottom and had the water churned up pretty good. I knew that if I took it at about 40 mph and stayed well to the left where the water was deeper, the mud wouldn't be rutted so badly. I wound 'er up and hit the hole in third gear with the engine revved right up so I would have lots of power.

The water was substantially deeper than I had thought; either that or the mud underneath was softer than I had anticipated. In any case, when we hit the water, the force of it blew the rusty floorboards right out from under our feet.

I had often thought it would be interesting to watch a waterbomber put on a load of water in a lake by dropping their scoop and skimming along the surface of the water. Now I'm not so interested. We experienced the same effect inside the cab of the truck with mud and slough water.

I was afraid of parking the truck out in the middle of the slough so I kept the pedal to the metal. I could tell by the feminine vocalizations in my right ear that the respect and admiration they had for me was waning.

We made it through the hole but when the water rushed back out through the nonexistent floor it took Mum's books and good humour with it. We looked down through what used to be the floor at the ground going by. It surprised me how much mud was continually being flung off the tires.

Shelby and Mum lifted their feet up onto the dash board to keep from falling through the floor but they were so mesmerized by what was happening that they forgot about the next water hole. We hit it at about 30 mph. With their feet up on the dash board, their open skirts were able to block most of the blast of mud so it wasn't nearly as bad as the first one was. I couldn't see a thing by then so I turned on the windshield wipers, but the mud was on the inside. I had to use the sleeve of my suit coat to wipe a hole I could see through.

We made it to the house and I got out and hid in the barn for the rest of the afternoon. It's been more than twenty years. I'll bet they laugh about it now.

Friends are God's apology for relations.
- Hugh Kingsmill

In your imagination, join me and my cousins as we sit on the floor around Great Grandpa's chair. He has been singing funny songs and telling us stories. When he starts telling us about laughing, he begins to laugh and as his story changes, so does his laugh until we are all holding our sides and laughing with him. He seems to be barely able to finish but suddenly he does and he is frowning and grumpy and wondering what we are laughing about.

*L*aughin'

    *L*aughing is the sensation of feeling good all over and showing it mainly in one spot. It is the next best thing to the Ten Commandments. It is the fireworks of the soul.

    Laughing is just as natural to come to the surface as a rat is to come out of his hole when he wants to. You can't keep it back by swallowing any more than you can the hiccups. If a man can't laugh then there is some mistake made in putting him together. And if he won't laugh, he needs just as much keeping away from as a bear trap does when it is set.

    There's some folks who laugh way too much for their own good or anybody else's. They laugh like a barrel of new cider with the bung pulled out - a perfect stream. Now this is a great waste of natural juice.

    Now there's other folks who don't laugh enough to give themselves vent. They're like a barrel of new cider too, all bunged up tight, liable to spring a hoop and leak away on the sly. There are neither of these two ways right and they never ought to have been patented.

    Genuine laughing is the vent of the soul, the nostrils of the heart and is just as necessary as spring weather is for a trout. There's one kind of laugh that I always did recommend. It looks out at the eyes first with a merry twinkle, then creeps off into the dimples of the cheeks and rides around those little whirlpools for awhile, then it lights up the whole face like a damask rose, then peals off into the air as clear and as happy as a dinner bell. Then it goes back on golden tip toe like an angel out for as errand and lies down in a bed of violets where it come from.

    Then there's the kind of a laugh nobody can withstand. It's as honest and as noisy as a district school let out to play. It shakes a man from his toes to his temples and twists him like a whiskey fit. It lifts him from his chair like feathers and lets him fall back again like lead. It goes all through him like a pickpocket and leaves him as weak and as crazy as if he was in a Russian bath all day and forgot to be took out.

    If you are laughin', open your mouth wide enough so the noise can get through without squeaking. Throw your head back like you're going to get shaved, hold on to your sides with both hands and then laugh until your soul feels thoroughly rested. In conclusion I say laugh every good chance you get, but don't laugh if you don't feel like it.

*F*riends

As a person goes through school, work and the other events of life, friends will come and go for various reasons. Some friends that we make in school and youth seem very important while we are young but as soon as school days are done, the friendship dies without a whimper. Some friends that we make have a lasting effect on us and the friendship remains strong through the years, even when distance makes association difficult.

As I think back of the many friends and acquaintances of my youth, there are several friends who have stood the test of time and distance.

The best friends I have now were mortal enemies when we were younger. Those friends are my brothers - Heath and Nathan (we called them Heathen Nathan), Quenton, Hayden and Andrew - and my sister Shelby. Now that we are older and have children of our own, they have become those whom I rely on most in times of crisis and they have yet to let me down. This may be just a ruse on their part to lull me into a false sense of security so they can make good their threat of years ago.

"We can't wait until you are an old geezer in a wheelchair and then we will come to the old folk's home and push you down the stairs."

They were always accusing me of some injustice. They would run off to Mum and tattle on me and I would have to explain to Mum, "It all started when Heath hit me back."

I swear, every time I broke Nathan's leg it was not very intentional. If he had been holding on tighter when the wagon hit that tree he wouldn't have fallen out and then when he got his cast off he shouldn't have had his leg under the carpet where I could jump out of bed on it. Nathan shouldn't have jumped off the raft like that, either, when we were so far from the shore. He didn't believe me when I told him that the raft always sank a little way like that. He should thank me for helping him learn how to swim instead of accusing me of nearly drowning him.

Then there was the time Mum got mad at us for wrecking the baby's plastic bathtub. We were using it for a sled for sliding down the stairs. Mum was worried that it would break and took it away from us. We were wondering what else we could use for a sled when I thought of using a cardboard box. We had used cardboard before for sliding on the snow and I could see no reason why it wouldn't work for sliding down the wooden stairs in the house. Heath was small enough to try it first. We put him in the box, shut the lid and pushed it down the stairs. It would have worked fine if the front edge of the box hadn't caught on the second step.

Heath had no trouble getting out of the box because it was all ripped and wrecked before he even got to the bottom but he still whined and cried

about it.

My Aunty Marian, or Beeno as I called her for the first few years, was the playmate I remember most until my school days. She was a year older than me and knew so much more than me. She was always telling me things that she knew.

"Those are telephone poles," she said pointing at a power line pole. "The voices travel down those wires to the other people's phones. Can you hear that humming noise? That is all the voices. If you stick your ear against the pole you can hear what they are saying."

We stuck our ears against the pole. She told me she could just about make out what they were saying. I told her I could hear something too.

She told me how Grandma would grow mashed potatoes by planting a potato and then stepping on it to mash it and then when they were finished growing you just picked them off the leaves and put them it a bowl. We looked under the leaves and sure enough there were some white fuzzy things stuck under the leaves. Marian said they weren't ripe yet and we couldn't pick them. I asked Grandma and she said they were called cocoons and that I shouldn't touch them because they had a worm inside it. Marian told me that of course it had a worm in it, worms liked mashed potatoes too, and you just had to pick the worm out before you poured the gravy on. I learned a lot of things from Marian that they don't teach you in school.

Marian and I got along really well between fights, but then as we started school she began hanging around kids who were in her grade and I was left behind. It wasn't long, though, before I started making friends of my own.

Jake showed up at about the same time as when I started school and we became close friends. It seemed as though trouble followed him around and I always wound up getting the worst of it.

Jim took Jake and me out on his horse. We were going to ride down to Alvin's place a half mile away. The snow was very deep and we were going across the field on the horse with all three of us riding bareback – Jim in front, me in the middle and Jake on behind. Jake fell off, taking me with him and we landed in the deep snow. Jim got off and put us both back on the horse and then crawled back on. We had only gone a few yards when Jake went off on the other side, pulling me off with him. Once more Jim had to get off and put us back on the horse.

The third time, Jake slid off clutching at the back of my coat and both of us landed in the snow. Jim left us laying there and rode back to the house. He came back a minute later with a length of baler twine. He put us both on the horse and then tied our feet together under the horse with the twine.

"There, that will keep you both on."

Ten yards further I felt Jake starting to slide off. I tried holding onto Jim but Jake was too heavy and off we went. Because the twine was still tied to our feet, we just rotated on the horse until we were dangling under the horse by our feet, with our heads dragging in the snow. Luckily the horse was a calm and quiet old mare that wasn't perturbed by two thrashing yelling boys hanging under her belly. Jim simply took his pocket knife and cut the twine and we were dropped right there in the snow under her feet. I have wondered how the horse avoided stepping on us. We were thrashing around like a couple of cats in a bag. Jim left us laying there and rode off and I missed my chance to go to Alvin's house. Jake and I had to walk almost a hundred yards back to the house.

Jake and I were blood brothers. We knew that to be blood brothers each of us had to cut the palm of our hand and then hold our hands together so the blood would be mingled and we would then be blood brothers forever. The thought of cutting the palm of our hands was a pretty serious thing, so the more we thought about it the more we thought that the important part was that there would be mingled blood, and that cutting your hand was something that you did if you were as tough as the Indians and cowboys of the movies. We weren't quite that tough when the time came so we each picked a scab and held the two sores together and that was the way we became blood brothers. We never told anybody because we were afraid we would become known as the Scab Brothers.

I was trying to teach Jake the finer arts of making a bomb one night at a Boy Scouts meeting and I was in the process of loading the bomb full of propellant when Jake asked me what he was supposed to do with the match. I told him that he was supposed to light the fuse with it.

I assumed that he knew I meant after I was done with the fuel. I was wrong. The resulting explosion blinded both of us momentarily and broke one of Jake's eardrums. Not to mention getting us both into trouble when the Scout Master came out and started asking pointed questions. Apparently there is no badge for bomb making.

Grandma and Grandpa Hatch had moved to Cardston when I was in grade eight and once in a blue moon, Mum and Dad would go for a visit. If these trips happened in the winter, I stayed home to feed cows and keep the fire going so the house wouldn't freeze up. Jake stayed with me a couple of times. That is where I learned not to trust Jake's cooking. One night we decided to have some canned beans for supper. We took the lids off of two cans and dumped them into two frying pans.

"That looks like quite a bit doesn't it?"

"Nah," says Jake. "My mum always cooks one can per person."

"Are you sure she uses forty eight ounce cans and not the little ones?"

"Maybe you're right. Ninety six ounces of beans does look like a lot."

It was too late then, we had to finish cooking them now that they were in the frying pans. Jake got a fork to stir with and he would stir the beans and then take the fork and scratch his head with it. He seemed to have only one itchy spot on his head because there was only one streak of beans along the side of his head just above his ear. The next morning we reheated the beans and ate some more.

I began to wonder if Jake's itchy spot was a simple case of dandruff or maybe it was the result of having a sampling of everything he ate dabbed on there because he was at it again, scratching his head with the fork. That evening we were able to finish the last of the beans. The after-effects of two boys eating beans three meals a day is not pleasant. When Mum came home she questioned us about it, and as punishment, she made us wash all our dishes.

Jake and I became connoisseurs of the woods. We had decided to sample all of the culinary delicacies the wild woods could provide.

We discovered that there is a reason why beef, chicken and pork became the staple meats. We began carrying a frying pan and a can of salt around behind the seat of my truck, and at every road kill we saw we would stop and see if it was fresh enough to eat. If it was, we would build a small fire in the ditch and cook it up. If it wasn't, we would throw it in the back of my truck with the intention of eventually skinning them in the spring when all had thawed, hoping for enough to make a fur coat.

We were quite worried one time when an RCMP officer stopped behind my truck which was parked on the shoulder of the highway. We had a road killed mink roasting on a fire. The mink had been eating a dead deer when he had been hit, so when the officer got out of his car and walked up beside the truck, he saw parts of a deer scattered across the road, a truck box full of dead skunks, rabbits, coyotes and other assorted creatures, and two connoisseurs preparing the day's entrée. He just stood and looked at us for awhile, and then waved, walked back to his car and left. We were relieved to know that we weren't breaking any laws.

Skunks taste just about how you would imagine. It was a total waste of time, especially after having stopped at about twenty before we found one that we could get close enough to pick up and skin out. Owls are unbelievably tough. Gophers are better in the fall than in the spring and even at best it takes about fifteen to make a meal. We finally gave up and decided that we liked our mother's cooking better than anything we had come up with.

I discovered something else, too, that hadn't crossed my mind. Girls aren't impressed with the idea of going on a date or having a fur coat when they see it in the raw state piled in the back of a pickup truck. Rhonda took one look in the back of my truck and decided that she wasn't feeling so good after all and should probably stay home and get her homework done. I emptied my truck but by then it was too late.

The night of my senior prom was not what you would expect if you knew all about prom night from watching Disney movies. After the graduation ceremonies were over, I picked up Jake and we went for pizza, then took my truck downtown. Jake was wearing a World War I leather pilot's helmet and a white scarf, I was wearing a white motorcycle helmet and a white scarf, and we 'cruised Main.'

As we drove down Main Street we would both jump out of the truck fifty yards before the four-way stop sign and grabbing hold on the truck bumper, bring it to a stop. Then, when the traffic cleared and it was our turn to go, Jake would get in the passenger's side and I would walk around to the front of the truck.

Jake would lean out the window and yell, "CONTACT!!"

I would yell, "CONTACT!!" and then grabbing an imaginary propeller, I would spin it as Jake started the truck.

From the sidewalk, people could not see how Jake was starting the truck as he was not reaching across to the key. He was simply using my own unique starter system. They had no choice but to believe that I was actually spinning an invisible propeller. The truck even sounded like an old Sopwith Camel airplane from 1915. It coughed and sputtered and sounded very authentic, and with us dressed up as pilots I'm sure the people on the sidewalk were very impressed as we took off into the cloud of blue smoke.

We made one mistake. We tried our starting procedure once in the school parking lot. I was spinning the invisible propeller while Jake, in the passenger's seat, started the truck. It was in reverse when it started, and before Jake could get over behind the wheel and stop it, the truck had run backwards down the hill from the parking lot and onto the highway. Luckily no one was coming or we would have been kind of embarrassed. There were quite a few people watching and they were very impressed. I could tell by the applause.

Darrell came to live in Cherry Grove when we were in grade three or four. We became good friends even though we were opposite in almost everything. I was short, he was tall; I was scrawny, he was the biggest and strongest kid all through school. He won all the academic awards in school, I won the teacher's praise when I got 51% on an exam. Darrell played sports, I played hooky. Darrell was a long distance runner, I got winded watching him. But despite our differences, we became close friends. Darrell, Jake and I became Cherry Grove's version of the Three Amigos.

With the combined efforts of all three of us working together, we were able to get ourselves out of many a scary predicament.

Darrell and I were one grade ahead of Jake and so the two of us spent our school days together. My mother was always comparing Darrell's school grades with mine. In grade seven she talked to the principal and had me put in the same class with Darrell, hoping that it would make a difference. No such luck. Darrell's grades still stayed at an A+ average.

Our teacher in grade seven didn't seem to like me very much and I reciprocated. He liked to have any offending student stand at the back of the class with a dictionary in each hand, arms stretched out to the side at shoulder height. As you stood there, your shoulders would start to burn and if you let your arms down he would holler at you to get them back up. This went on until you couldn't hold them up anymore and then he would let you go back to your seat.

It didn't take me long to figure out that the longer I stood there holding those books up, the less notes I had to take. So one morning I snuck into the class room and put two small nails in the wall so that when my arms were outstretched, I could hook my shirt sleeves at both wrists onto the nails and the nails would hold my arms up. The teacher soon discovered that I didn't have my homework done and sent me to the back to hold dictionaries.

I held the books out and stood with my back against the wall and my arms held by my sleeves on the nails. The teacher kept looking at me, wondering when my arms would give out and I would just glare at him. He let me stand there the entire class. I never had to hold dictionaries again but I don't know if it was because he found the nails or thought that if I could stand there all class, it wasn't punishment enough.

Darrell and I discovered Leonardo Da Vinci in grade seven and were fascinated by how smart he was. The most impressive thing to us was that Da Vinci wrote his notes in mirror image, meaning that you had to hold them to a mirror to read them. So Darrell and I thought that if we could do that then we would be as smart as Leonardo Da Vinci.

I sacrificed many hours of homework to master the art of writing backwards, but it finally paid off. Both Darrell and I got so that we could write our notes in mirror image as fast as we could write properly. In fact, my writing was more legible in the mirror than it was when writing normally. For some reason this was very important. I can't think of the reason right at the moment but I swear that there was a logical explanation.

Darrell and I loved to go up into the hills north of Cherry Grove and survive. We imagined ourselves as Boy Scouts extraordinaire, and we would go hiking and camping armed with no more than a pocket knife and a couple matches. We would set out determined to live off the land, eating the edible flora and snaring the edible fauna of the forest for our sustenance. There were times when we survived for several hours at a time before some unforeseen circumstance forced us to go home for some sandwiches.

As we participated in the Boy Scout program we went camping or canoeing whenever we could arrange it. We spent time in the bush learning about the predominant species of wildlife in the Cherry Grove area: mosquitoes.

Mosquitoes are a game bug but they won't bite at a hook. But there are still millions of them caught every year and this makes the market very unstable as the supply exceeds the demand. The song of the Mosquito is monotonous to some people, but in me it stirs up the memory of other days. Why, I've laid awake all night long many a time listening to the sweet little buzz of the Mosquito.

I discovered that in Cherry Grove, either the snow flies or black flies.

There were camps where there were no mosquitoes or black flies. Thoses were the camps when it was -40 degrees. It seems as though we would plan a camp and the day before we left, a cold front would blow in and the temperature would drop twenty degrees. This happened in the wintertime, too. I've spent nights on the beach on Cold Lake under a tarp in August wondering if it was going to stop raining and start snowing.

Darrell and I woke up one morning in a camp north of the Martineau River and the thermometer read -47 degrees Fahrenheit. My Uncle Darnell was the scout leader and we had to jack up the front of his truck and light a fire under the oil pan to get it started. Through all of our camps and activities Darrell and I worked together on achievement badges that we could sew onto our Scout shirt. Darrell earned almost every badge there was to earn and was awarded a gold chain and other awards. I, on the other hand, got a badge for gardening. I think that Uncle Darnell liked Darrell better than he liked me.

Darrell, Jake and I went on several Scout camps. The most notable was a Canadian Scout Jamboree in Prince Edward Island. As we took off on the big jet leaving Edmonton, the jet lifted off the runway and seemed to go up at an impossibly steep angle. I was sure that the pilot was going to miss a shift and power out and we would go rolling back down the hill.

The first evening at the jamboree there was a large opening ceremony held in an open field just down the hill from our tents. We could see and hear well enough from where we were so there was no reason to join the huge crowd that was sitting in front of a large stage. The Master of Ceremonies welcomed all the Scouts from across Canada and went on at some length about how safety should be our first concern. They then set off some fireworks to start the celebrations, one of which tipped over and shot straight into the crowd of boys. The fireworks stopped and in a minute an ambulance came and three boys were carried off on stretchers.

Jake, Robert and I were in one tent, and the combined effects of eating beans, not changing socks or underwear, and not bathing during ten days of hard physical activity had made the interior of the tent the equivalent of a tear gas attack. Our tent had to be burned when we got home because even after days of airing it out, the smell was too overpowering to be endured by anything less than a skunk with sinus problems.

Darrell built a dune buggy that I have never forgiven him for. My Uncle Ed had a Volkswagen Beetle that was sitting at Uncle Byron's place and had been for a few months. I was working for Ed one summer and thought that the Volkswagen would be a wonderful addition to the fleet of vehicles I had been amassing. The reason being it ran. So I offered Ed a sum of money that was more than the car was worth and he agreed. I paid him in cash and he wrote me a receipt. I had Ed drop me off at Byron's to get the car. I walked out behind Byron's barn to where it was parked and there it was, gone. I went into Byron's and asked him where the Volkswagen had gone.

"I sold it to Darrell."

I went to Darrell's and asked him about the car.

"Ya. I have it," Darrell said, "I asked Byron how much he wanted for it and he only wanted a dollar. I gave him a dollar and he wrote out a receipt and then gave me the dollar back."

I explained to Darrell that it was Ed's car and not Byron's, and that I had bought it from Ed. I even offered to give Darrell another dollar for it but he had already cut the body off of it and was turning it into a dune buggy. I went to Ed and tried to get my money back.

It seems that Ed owed Byron money and if I was willing to pay Byron the fifty dollars that Ed owed him, Byron was willing to call it even, give me the receipt, and I could go to Darrell and get my dollar back.

Darrell built his dune buggy by stripping the body off of it and by modifying a Model T Ford body to fit it. He worked on it for quite a few months. It took a lot of hard work and engineering on Darrell's part to get it running just right. Just a few weeks after he got it finished he let Steve take it for a spin. I never heard the entire story of the accident but it will suffice to say that it never ran again, and I never even got to ride in it.

Now many years have gone by and Jake and Darrell have turned into a couple of old geezers with more kids than hair. But when we get together we still have enough of the old skills to enable us to shame our wives and embarrass our children.

There is an old proverb that Hans Christian Anderson is given credit for. The truth of the matter is that he misquoted a saying that has been in the Hatch family for many generations. The misquotation has been perpetuated down through the years and this record of my family has been written to set the record straight and give credit where credit is due.

The Battle

Far away in ancient day, a clan there was named Hatch.
A numerous clan of brawny men, nay the county had nay match.
Now old Lord Hatch was a baron cruel, and the peasants were afraid.
They slaved away in the field all day and little were they paid.

The many sons and brothers of the clan on the estate
Spent their day in sport and play, whilst the peasants worked till late.
But then one day, one dreadful day, a horde of Vikings came,
And landed on the rugged shore and brought the clan full shame.

A whole boat load of horn-ed men had come to loot and pillage.
The peasant folk to Lord Hatch quoth, "Pray come and save our village.
"They're brutal men ne'er brush their teeth. They fight and drink all night".
The only meat they ate was raw, for their barbeque would nay light.

Wild they were, bloodthirsty too, and on their chests was hair.
On this voyage long they'd only packed one change of underwear.
Old Lord Hatch, how brave was he, he faced the Viking king.
"A battle!" cried he, "A challenge for thee, let the field of battle ring!"

"I have no fear of thee, "quoth he, "and of thy men I'm not.
"And we will leave thy scurvy bones on the battlefield to rot."
"Of Donald's sons we've seventeen, of David's sons there's nine.
And of the sons of Fredrick Hatch two score, and then there's mine."

"Why should we fear thy motley crew, we'll have thee on the run.
"With all our clan that will bear arms we out number thee three to one."
So there they met on the field of war, the Vikings and the clan,
They took one look at the Viking horde and they all turned tail and ran.

There stood Lord Hatch all by himself, with his old tin sword and shield,
To face, alone, that Viking crowd which stood upon the field .
Brief it was, the battle that day, and man, he took a lickin'
The moral my lad, is ne'er count your Hatches before they chicken.

Grade Three

By the time I got to grade three I considered myself pretty well educated. I knew all the numbers up to R, and when we sang the numbers to the tune of Twinkle, Twinkle Little Star, I could get all the way to Z. There was one number though that had me stumped. It was the one between K and P. It was pronounced "ellymennoe", it must be a pretty big number to have such a long name.

Mrs. Himmelsbach was my teacher and she would tell the class that we would be learning rithmatic, and how to do addition and distraction. I had never heard of those things before so I wasn't interested and looked out of the window. There was a pair of barn swallows building a nest. They would fly away and return in a few minutes with a mouth full of mud and stick it to a spot on the eaves trough just outside the window from where I sat. It was fascinating to watch them flying back and forth. In a matter of just a few hours they had enough mud stuck to the eaves trough that they started to bring grass, twigs, string and other assorted things to line their nest with. I watched them all morning as they struggled to build a home for the eggs that were sure to come. At recess I went outside and found a stick that I could use to knock down the nest.

After recess Mrs. Himmelsbach told us that we were going to learn about Dick and Jane. We took out our Dick and Jane readers.

Dick could run fast. Jane could run fast. Dick was unaware that the swallows were back and rebuilding the nest. They had moved over a little bit and were once again sticking mud to the eaves trough. It was gross how they would cough up a ball of mud and stick it onto the last little mud ball they had left. Eventually the nest looked as though it was made of hundreds of little chicken turds all stuck together.

One of the swallows flew over to the middle of the play ground and found a string that it tried to pick up but the string was too heavy. I was worried for a minute that he would haul it away because I recognized the string. It was one of my shoe laces. I had left it out there tied to a stick with the other end in a loop around a gopher hole. I glanced at the clock. It was still more than two numbers away from dinner time and Dick was still jumping and running fast.

I looked back out the window and that darn swallow had moved my string and the gopher had popped out of his hole and the noose hadn't caught him. I looked at the clock again. It wasn't moving. I wondered if I should point out to Mrs. Himmelsbach that the clock was not moving and we might be missing lunch time. Jane was still doing something of little importance so I watched to see which hole the gopher went down so that as soon as the bell rang I could get out and redo my noose around the right hole. After about fifteen hours the lunch bell finally rang.

The playground was very large and had some very tall grass and trees around the perimeter. Not enough to be called a forest, but enough that a small boy could hide in the grass and take his shoe laces out. I would tie them end to end and make a small noose at one end, creating a miniature lariat. Sneaking out of the grass like a panther after a small prey I would creep out and put the noose around the opening of one of the hundreds of gopher holes that dotted the playground. I would then slip back into the tall grass and wait there, peeking out at the hole, waiting for a gopher to show his head. A quick jerk on the shoelace and you had him. But with so many kids out on the playground the gophers weren't showing.

All I needed was patience. I knew that before long the bell would ring and all the noisy kids would go away. Sure enough the bell soon rang and all the kids lined up to go back into the school. Hidden in the long grass, I knew that now the gopher would come out for sure. I waited. I could hear the gopher's little high pitched bark as they signaled to each other that the coast was clear. Any moment now he would show his head.

Then some teacher was outside yelling about something. "Shhhh!!" I thought. "He's almost there!"

Then more teachers and the principal were walking around the playground yelling and keeping all the gophers down. One teacher stopped almost on top of my gopher hole and yelled, "Did you find him yet!?"

It made me so mad. What was the use of hiding for so long if some bungling teacher is going to stand on top of the hole yelling? Finally she went away.

The gopher's head showed for an instant and I jerked the string. He darted back down the hole but I had been too fast for him and hauled him out kicking and swinging on the end of my string.

In the trees there was a spot where Shane and I had been making a fire during recess and there was lots of dry grass and small twigs just right for making fires. In no time at all I had a little fire going, and with a coat hanger that had been straightened out for just this purpose, I branded my gopher with a **TH** on the left hip.

I turned him loose and set my trap again. The teachers had gone away so it wasn't long before I had another one caught.

HORRORS!!!

Rustlers had been at my herd. Shane had obviously caught this one before. My **TH** brand had been blotted out and a big **S** was now branded on the gopher's' ribs. There was only one way to deal with a rustler. I took my hot coat hanger and blotted out the **S** and branded him on the other side with a **TH**. I had about twenty five head in my herd already but Shane was not playing by the rules. We had agreed that we would not brand the other's gophers. We had started out working together but after the very first gopher we had split up the partnership. I had put my brand (**TRAVIS HATCH**) on one side, and when he started to put his brand on the other side, the gopher died. He accused me of killing the gopher with too big of a brand but the gopher was fine when he got it. I think it died because he was stepping on it to hold it still. I wasn't going to hold it and get bit like he did when I was putting on my brand.

The gophers were getting pretty shy and harder to catch nowadays, and the bell rang for afternoon recess before I could catch another one. Some other kids were kicking a ball around so I went to play with them. Mrs. Himmelsbach saw me kicking the ball and came running over and hugged me.

"Oh Travis!" she cried. "I am so glad you're here!"

I always liked Mrs. Himmelsbach more than my other teachers. She was the only one who was ever glad to see me.

When recess was over we went back in and I watched some ants that were crawling in and out of a hole in the baseboard.

I learned quite a bit that year. Patrick had hair on his legs. He was the only one in grade three that did. He told me that when I was thirteen I would have hair on my legs too. I also discovered that swallows will only try three times to build a nest in the same spot before they give up and leave you with nothing to do during rithmatic class.

I learned other interesting things too. When someone sharpens their pencil and turns the crank five times, it won't be enough and they will have to stick it back in and crank some more. But if they crank it seven times, their pencil will have a perfect point. Ten cranks is almost certain to break the point off, and they will have to try again. Some kids sharpen their pencil twice a day and some kid's pencils only last two days because they keep cranking the sharpener more than seven times. My pencil always lasted a long time. I could never figure out why some kids had to sharpen their pencil two or more times in a day while my pencil stayed sharp for days at a time.

    Sometimes Mrs. Himmelsbach would interrupt my studies and ask me a question like, "Travis, do you know what page we are on?"

    I was usually right on top of it and within a minute or two I could tell her.

    I very rarely had to worry about my grades. I knew that Mrs. Himmelsbach talked to my mother on a regular basis and Mum would certainly let me know some time in June when I had to start worrying. Even at that, Mum seemed to worry more than I did.

Rule #1 at Hatch reunions:
Never let the facts interfere with a good story.

The Chocolate Milk Machine

*I*n the hallway of the elementary school, right by the principal's office, was a big red machine that looked like a deep freeze. On the front of it was a silver colored box with a slot in it where wealthy kids could stick a quarter. The machine would make a buzzing noise then a metallic click. The wealthy kid would then pull the lever on the lid and the lid would open. The wealthy kid would reach in and pull out a small carton of chocolate milk. He would shake it for a few seconds and then fold back the top of the carton to open it. I could see the little vapors that came off the outside of the carton, making it look like a frosty cold ice cream carton. There would be a dark brown foam on the top of the milk from shaking it. He would raise the carton to his lips and let the cool brown nectar slide down his tongue. He would invariably have a brown little mustache that he would lick off his upper lip with his tongue.

Day after day I watched as one lucky kid after another would stick in their quarter and pull out a carton of the most delicious looking chocolate milk. Some of those kids dropped in a quarter as if they had an endless supply of quarters and that having such a treat was an everyday thing. I even think that there may have been a couple of kids who had one every day, but I knew how much quarters were worth and I could hardly accept that someone could be so rich as to have a whole quarter to spend every day. That chocolate milk looked so good, though, that I couldn't think of anything better for a millionaire to spend his money on.

One day a radical thought entered my head. What if…? Just, what if Mum would give me a quarter? I knew what the answer would be before I asked, but the thoughts of that silky sweet brown nectar was more than my little heart could bear.

"Please Mum? Just one quarter?"

The answer was just as I expected, but I was disappointed none the less. Chocolate milk was a treat to be saved for Christmas or a birthday, and we couldn't afford to spend that much just for a school lunch.

I went back to school and each day stood by the water fountain across the hall as those wealthy kids drank chocolate milk right in front of me, as if to just rub it in that I had to drink plain old, cheap, affordable water.

I couldn't bear it any longer. I begged and pleaded with my mother for a quarter. Every day I would tell her how I suffered to see all that chocolate milk being wasted on such ingrates who could never appreciate it like I would. I told her how being left out of such bliss would scar me for life.

Finally my mother succumbed to my tears and pleading and gave me a quarter. A whole shiny quarter! I put it under my pillow and slept with my hand on it all night. In the morning I was so excited I was ready for the bus on time. It was as though Christmas had come early. The quarter was in my pocket and I kept sticking my hand in my pocket to touch it and make sure it was still there. I stood on the sidewalk all through recess not daring to play because I might lose my quarter. The morning dragged on and on and it seemed as though the clock wasn't moving.

At last the moment had come. I walked up to the machine nonchalantly, as though it were something I did every day. I certainly didn't want other kids thinking that this was my first time getting a chocolate milk. I reached into my pocket for the quarter and pulled it out. Holding it between my thumb and forefinger I reached out and let it fall into the slot. I could almost taste the cool dark chocolate. The quarter fell clinking into the machine. I waited for the buzz and click. It was silent. I tried the handle.

It wouldn't move. I tried it again.

Nothing.

I stood there dumbfounded. The principal opened the door and asked, "What are you doing?"

I thought he would give me the strap if he found out that someone had wrecked the machine, so I ran.

I ran until I was out in the tall grass where no one could see me and I thought about my quarter until my sleeve got wet from wiping away the thoughts of that stupid quarter.

My children have often wondered why I give them a hard time about guzzling too much chocolate milk. I guess it is because I still think that a quarter is too much to spend on plain old good for nothing chocolate milk.

*T*eam *D*rivers

*M*arian and I learned to drive at the same time. This does not mean that we went to driving school together. It means that it took both of us working together at the same time to drive one truck. When Marian was about six years old and I was about five, we learned to drive a pickup truck. Neither one of us was big enough to see over the dashboard and touch the pedals at the same time so we learned to team drive. Marian knelt on the seat, operated the steering wheel and shifted the gears. I sat on the floor under the steering wheel and operated the pedals. Marian got to do the steering because she could punch harder than me.

Together we became quite a team and could drive virtually anywhere. We started out in the fields hauling hay with Jim and Ed. Marian would give directions: "Okay, go."

I would step on the clutch pedal and Marian would move the gear lever to first gear. I then let out the clutch and stepped on the gas pedal. It wasn't the smoothest operation to begin with but it wasn't long before we were as smooth as most people.

"Shift!"

I would let off the gas and step on the clutch, Marian would then shift the gear lever to second. In this manner we would drive all over the farm.

One day Marian and I were driving the truck for Jim and Ed's hay hauling. Jim and Ed had invited Barb to come along with them so they could show her what manly guys they were as they threw the bales on and off the truck. Barb came along and sat on the top of the load of hay and admired their big muscles and laughed at their witty remarks.

Marian was kneeling on the seat as usual, giving directions and steering, and I was on the floor under the steering wheel running the pedals. We would drive in first gear across the field, stopping at each stook of hay bales. When we stopped Jim or Ed would jump off the truck and throw the bales onto the truck, the other would stay on the truck and stack the bales. When all the bales in that stook were on the truck, they would yell to us and we would drive to the next stook. When the truck had a full load we would drive back to the barn yard where they would unload the truck and stack the hay in a large stack by the feed yard.

Everyone was having a grand time until Marian decided that she was big enough to drive all by herself. I crawled up and sat on the seat next to her with my feet hardly reaching past the edge of the seat. When Jim called to go to the next stook, Marian slid down under the steering wheel until she could reach the pedals. Her chin was just about even with the bottom of the steering wheel. Jim and Ed got on the back of the truck. Marian put the transmission in second gear, pushed the gas pedal right to the floor and let out the clutch. Jim and Ed got off the truck, along with half the load of hay. Marian could no more see where she was going than a goat can sing opera, but she was making good time.

All of a sudden, I was surprised to see a face with a gargoyle-like expression looking in through the top of the windshield. Barb was still on top of the load and was lying on her stomach on the top of the cab, looking down through the windshield. She started pounding on the windshield, screaming at Marian to stop. Marian stopped. Barb did not.

I watched as Barb shot off the roof of the truck and skipped off the hood like a flat stone on the water with her arms and legs spread eagle. She disappeared over the front of the truck and I remember thinking that she wasn't going to fly very far with her arms held out rigidly like that. Why, they weren't even flapping. Her lips, on the other hand, seemed as though they wouldn't quit.

The problem as we saw it was that no one let us drive anywhere except on the farm. It was almost as though they didn't trust us or something. After all if we were old enough to go to school, surely we were old enough to be trusted on the highways too, right?

But even though we put on many miles on the farm, we were never allowed to experience the thrill of the open road. That was, until everyone left one weekend to go to Edmonton and left Marian and I to do the babysitting. She was about nine or ten by that time and we had become accomplished team drivers, so when we saw a coyote out on the field there was little hesitation to get in the truck and go chase it. We saw nothing wrong with that. All five of the little kids were safe because they were with us. We wouldn't do anything as foolish as leave a bunch of little kids alone. They could get into trouble.

Chasing the coyotes was fun but not as fun as driving to Cherry Grove to the store for some pop or gum. We searched around and found some empty bottles we could return at the store for a refund and took off for the store. We knew we weren't allowed to drive on the highway but we reasoned that as long as we drove down the railroad grade we could get all the way to Cherry Grove without driving on the highway. The gravel road between Grandma's and the highway didn't count as a road because we didn't think about it very hard.

We loaded our bottles and the other kids in the truck and headed to Cherry Grove. With me sitting on the floor, I could see nothing, but knew we were going pretty fast. We had only gotten the truck into high gear a few times before. This time Marian was telling me to go faster so I stepped on the gas a little harder.

"How fast are we going, Marian?"

"About fifty."

In those days every thing was in miles per hour so we were traveling about 80 kmh down a narrow gravel road.

"Isn't that a little fast?"

"Why? Dad drives this fast all the time."

We turned off the road onto the railroad grade. Many years before my time, a railroad had been planned and construction begun on a railway between Grande Centre and Pierceland. The grade had been built but then abandoned before any rail was laid. The grade was parallel to the highway for many miles through Cherry Grove and was used quite often for vehicle traffic, farm machinery, etc. It wasn't as smooth as a road but Marian was still able to hold the truck on the grade at about fifty miles per hour. We stopped at the store, did our shopping and headed for home by the same route.

Each subsequent trip to the store that day was made for a lesser and lesser reason until I'm sure that the term joyriding might have been a better description of our activities. We never forgot our responsibilities in regards to the little kids though, and kept them with us all day where they would be safe.

I believe that there may have been some discussion of the matter between our parents and Marian but for some reason I was not involved in them. I assume it was because Marian was a year older than me and she should have known better. I always knew that when we got in trouble it was her fault anyway. I, being the younger of the two of us, was always the innocent victim of her evil influences on me.

Cowboy's Dream

Every eye was on her
As she walked in through the door.
My heart it stopped its beating.
She was what I'd waited for.

Her coal black hair, her soft brown eyes,
Her face as white as cream,
The way she walked with her long legs
Was every cowboy's dream.

Then she stopped. Her eyes met mine.
She slowly walked my way.
My hand reached out to touch her cheek
But she shyly moved away.

No words passed between us
But I'm sure she knew
That she'd be mine regardless
Of what others say or do.

So many times I'd been there
And so many times I'd lost.
This time I knew that she'd be mine
No matter what the cost.

My hand went up of its own accord.
I heard someone speak my name.
I also bought her calf at side
For one-ten a hundred weight.

*H*elping *D*ad

*W*hen I was four years old I thought my dad was so cool. I thought that there was no one that was as smart and strong as my dad. The most cool thing about my Dad was his Adam's apple. It stuck out of the front of his neck like an armadillo climbing a rope. I was always amazed that he never choked on it. I remember sitting in church fascinated by Dad's Adam's apple, counting how many times he swallowed during the meeting. Dad had other noteworthy abilities. He could cut a full sized pancake in half and then eat the whole thing in two bites. Only a real hero could do something like that.

I remember Dad's birthday when he turned 25. It was then I realized just how ancient he was too. I'd heard about fossils and knew that they were really old too and thought that if my dad was 25 he was probably as old as any other fossil. He got a pair of cowboy boots for his birthday and he let me try them on. They came half way up my thigh but clomping around in those boots, why, I couldn't wait to grow up and wear a pair just like them.

My dad could do anything too. One day I went out to play and Dad was laying underneath the car. The front wheels of the car were up on two big blocks and Dad was underneath with only his feet showing.

"Whatcha doin', Dad?"

"Fixing the car."

"What's this thing, Dad?"

"That's the oil pump."

The oil pump was a cool looking thing with a pipe and a screen on one end. I had a great idea and took it over to the sand box. It worked great. I could scoop up some sand and pour it in the screen. The dry sand would pour out the end of the pipe and the lumps that the cats always buried in the sand were left on the screen. The dry lumps I could crush up with my fingers but the soft ones weren't good for anything so I put them in my pocket. I went back and crawled under the car to see what Dad was doing.

"What's that thing for, Dad?"

He started to tell me, so I collected some more stuff he had dropped and went back to the sandbox. When I came back he was still talking to me so I crawled up onto the top of the motor. There was a big hole in the top of the motor.

"What's this, Dad?"

He told me it was the garborator so I pulled out all the lumps I had in my pocket and threw them in.

I helped Dad all day until Mum made me go in the house and get ready for bed. I laid in bed that night listening to Mum and Dad talking. I couldn't get to sleep for the longest time because Dad was telling Mum about "that little rat" that had ruined his oil pump. I knew that rats were great big mice that chewed on things and one must have been right there close by the sandbox watching for me to drop that oil pump so he could chew it. I was worried. What if the rat was there tomorrow? What if he came when I was there?

Dad sounded really upset. Maybe he saw the rat. He must have, because I could hear him yelling that if he caught that rat doing it again he was going to choke him.

The next morning Dad said he wanted to talk to me. He talked for a long time while I watched his Adam's apple going up and down. I counted up to eleventeen times. He asked me if I understood.

I said, "Yes. You don't want cat herds in the motor." He seemed content with that answer, so I went out to the sandbox to play but I kept an eye out for the rat.

The next summer when I was five, my uncles were down helping Dad haul hay. We had two hay wagons. I went with Uncle Byron and Jim out to the field where they loaded up the wagon with small square bales. The wagon was pulled by the John Deere R tractor. When the wagon was full, Uncle Byron pushed the hand clutch in and the tractor started moving. Uncle Byron let me stand in front of the seat and steer the tractor as we went back to the yard. When we got back, we unhooked the full wagon and hooked onto the empty wagon. Dad and Ed would unload the full one and stack the hay while Byron and I went back to the field for another load.

Once the second wagon was loaded, Byron pushed in the clutch and then jumped off the tractor. He shouted at me, "When you get to the yard just pull the clutch lever back and it will stop."

It was at that moment that I knew I would be a farmer just like my dad. There was no greater feeling in the world than to be sitting up there in control of all that power. Why, that tractor had so much power that it never even hesitated when the wagon hit the gate post. When I got back to the yard I drove straight toward the hay stack. When I judged that I was getting close enough I let go of the steering wheel, grabbed the clutch lever and pulled it. It didn't move. I used both hands and pulled again. It didn't move. I was getting close enough so that I could see Dad's Adam's apple bobbing up and down as his mouth moved. It was moving very quickly. I grabbed the lever with both hands and braced both feet against the dashboard and pulled for all I was worth. The lever popped into neutral and the tractor stopped.

Dad then did something that I have never forgotten. He said nothing but unhooked the wagon, backed the tractor around, hooked up the empty wagon, pushed the clutch lever in and jumped off. As I drove back out to the field I knew that my dad could see I was finally a grownup and could be trusted like a real man. There was only one or two other times when my dad made me feel that good again.

Mum, on the other hand, blew it when she came out and caught me driving the tractor by myself. The way she carried on you would think we were doing something dangerous. I think Byron and Dad caught the worst of it and she wouldn't trust me on a tractor by myself again until I was way older. I think I was almost seven before I learned to run the hay rake.

The summer I was eight I earned Dad's trust again, or it could be that he was desperately shorthanded. Anyway, he gave me instructions on how to run the baler tractor. He told me which lever to pull to go faster and which one to slow down and how to stop. Away we went and he jumped onto the stooker. Dad was doing his best to stook the hay while at the same time coach me over the roar of the tractor and baler which way to turn and whether to slow down or speed up.

I found it very difficult to watch him all the time and still drive straight along beside the swath. His high decibel driving instructions were distracting me and I would not see a big wad of hay and it would plug the baler. We would have to stop and I would wait while Dad unplugged the baler and put in a new shear bolt. We would go for another few feet and he would distract me and there we would be waiting on him again. Finally after an hour or two Dad said he only had one more shear bolt left which meant that I'd better go run the rake again. I liked that job better anyway. There were no distractions and I could drive a lot straighter.

I went with my Dad whenever I could. It didn't matter what he was doing. I especially liked riding on the tractor, and would spend hours riding along watching whatever piece of equipment we happened to be pulling. Dad would often let me steer and it was thrilling. As I grew older, driving tractor was one job that I loved to do. I would tell Mum on school mornings when Dad was gone, "The harrowing on the big field should really be done today or Dad will be behind when he gets home."

Every once in awhile Mum would give in and let me stay home and drive tractor putting the crop in or hauling hay or something. My school marks were always in the fifties so it wasn't like I was behind or anything, but she worried none the less.

Betsy and the Bar

In a farmer's cabin out west, so they say,
A great grizzly bear traveled one day
And seating himself upon the hearth
Commenced to eat the contents
Of a two gallon pan of milk and potatoes,
An excellent meal,
Then looked around to see what he could steal.

> The Lord of the mansion awoke from his sleep
> And hearing the ruckus he ventured to peep
> Just out in the kitchen to see what was there,
> And was scared to behold a great grizzly bear.
> With a cry of alarm to his slumbering frau,
> "There's a bar in the kitchen as big as a cow!"
> "A what?" "Why a bar." "Well murder him then."
> "Well I will, my dear Betsy, if you first venture in."

So Betsy jumped up and the poker she seized.
Her man shut the door and against it he squeezed.
Poor Betsy then laid on the bruin her blows,
First on the forehead and then on the nose.
Her man through the keyhole kept shouting within,
"Well done my brave Betsy now hit him agin.
"Now a jab in the ribs, now a poke on the snout,
"Now take that old poker and poke his eyes out!"

> So rapping and poking, poor Betsy alone
> At last laid poor bruin as dead as a stone.
> He hastened to the neighbours, the story to tell
> The wonderful things the morning befell.
> How "me and my Betsy just slaughtered a bar
> "Yes all you neighbours come and see, we did it,
> "Yep me and my Betsy we did it."

Revenge

    Some bullies begin exercising their muscle and persecuting those around them at a very young age. My sufferings began under the hand of a three year old girl named Aunty Marian. Oh, how I suffered through my early years, and the only reason I can write this story without fear of reprisal is the fact that she is now a geriatric old biddy and I'm almost sure I could take her now in a fair fight.

    It all started in the bathtub. Water was scarce in those days and in the winter we had to melt snow for bath water. At least that is the excuse Mum used when she made me bath with Marian. Marian was about three, I was about a year younger but I remember the humiliation of being subjected to the clutches of such a tyrant as my Aunty Marian. We had two toys that we could play with in the tub, a blue aluminum cup and a toy that my Grandpa had made out of a wooden thread spool, a rubber band and a stick. The spool was a wonderful toy, we would wind it up and it would go all by its self across the floor, or if played with in the tub it would spin soapy water right into my eyes. Marian and I could both sit in the galvanized wash tub with our legs stretched out and still have room to play with the cup and spool.

    As you've already guessed, Marian always got the spool and I didn't want the cup unless Marian had it. She would wind up the spool with the rubber band and hold onto the stick and when she let go of the spool it would spin very quickly and Marian would hold it in the water just deep enough that it would spray soapy water in my eyes. Or she would take the cup and pour water on my head. It was terrible and still haunts my memories, so I started plotting my revenge.

    Gum, or to be more specific, bubble gum was a treat that was had very rarely. It was terribly expensive and cost a whole penny for only one piece. Each piece of bubble gum came in a paper wrapper and underneath the wrapper was another little piece of paper that had a cartoon or a joke on it. Each piece of gum was treasured and horded and chewed until the teacher caught you with it and made you spit it out. When going to bed, one always stuck one's gum on the bed post where it could be readily had in the morning.

I had been chewing one piece when I was lucky enough to find a pop bottle under the seat of somebody's car at church. It wasn't empty when I found it, but because empty bottles were so valuable, I poured out the pop and then it was empty. The next time I was at the store I turned in the bottle and got two cents for it. With those two pennies I bought two more pieces of gum. The safest place for gum was in my mouth so those two pieces joined the one that was already there. That afternoon Grandma told us we had to have a nap, so Marian and I laid down on the couch for a nap.

When I woke up my gum was gone. I looked everywhere for it. I found a piece under the cushion of the sofa but it wasn't mine. I could tell because mine didn't have lint on it and mine tasted way better. I was heartbroken, three pieces of gum and I only got to chew it for a little while. It was not to be found.

Then Marian woke up and found it. She had stolen it, and had stuck it in her hair while we were sleeping! I had spent all of Sunday School looking for that bottle. The flavor wasn't even gone yet and she had it. I hadn't even gotten the joke that was under the wrapper, so I started plotting my revenge.

I knew that doctors always have a little rubber hammer that they use to test your kneeflexes. So I got a hammer from beside the anvil in Grandpa's basement. I held it behind my back and asked Marian if she had ever been to a doctor. She said she had but I didn't believe her. I asked her if she wanted to pretend we were at the doctor's. She said okay, so I said in my deepest doctor's voice, "Alright young lady, sit right here and cross your legs and I'll test your kneeflexes."

She did and I tested them with the hammer, but not quite hard enough because she caught me by the time I got to the bottom of the basement stairs and she started using her fists to test my headflexes and noseflexes. So I started plotting my revenge.

We liked to play hide-and-seek, and Grandma's house was full of cool places to hide. Behind the big chair in the living room was a hole in the floor exactly the size of one square tile. A scrawny little kid such as myself could scoot through the hole and drop down onto the mountain of dirty clothes that were always there in the girls' room. This was almost a necessity when playing with Marian because she cheated when she was 'It', and when she was supposed to count to a hundred to give us time to hide she would count by fives or tens and would catch me before I had a chance to even get out of the room. With the hole in the floor, I could be downstairs in a matter of a few seconds and have plenty of time to hide. Marian counted by tens, then twenties and still couldn't catch me. When it was my turn to be 'It' I started counting as fast as I could and Marian disappeared. When I got to a hundred I ran down to the basement as fast as I could and began looking. I found Kay hiding in the boys' closet and the two of us started looking for Marian. We looked in the root cellar and through every other room including the girls' room and couldn't find Marian.

After about a half hour of looking, we had to holler, "Come out, come out wherever you are!"

We heard the faintest little squeak, "Right here!"

But we couldn't tell where it came from so we ran upstairs.

"Where are you!!?" we yelled.

"Girls' room," came the squeak.

We ran back down to the girl's room and looked again and could see nothing.

"Up here," said the squeak.

We looked up at the ceiling to see Marian hanging head down from the hole. She had tried to go through the hole and had gotten stuck at the hips. The blood had been pooling in her head so long that her face looked like a scarlet jack-o-lantern.

"Why didn't you say something?" Kay asked her.

"I was winning," she whimpered. "Get me out."

Kay ran upstairs to get Grandma and the two of them moved the big chair and grabbed Marian's legs. I stayed downstairs with Marian.

Grandma said, "On the count of three, pull as hard as you can."

When Grandma counted three I grabbed Marian's arms and pulled as hard as I could, but Grandma and Kay were too much for me and they soon had her out.

Marian, when she could talk again, claimed that she was the winner but I maintained that she hadn't really hidden but had just gotten stuck so it didn't count. Kay then sided with Marian and then Marian called me a cry baby, so I began plotting my revenge.

"Wanna play again?" I asked her.

I knew that if I was patient enough she would eventually hide in the piano. Grandma's piano was a huge old upright Grand. In the front, under the key board, was a hidden lever that opened a sliding door at the bottom of the face plate under the keyboard. When the door was open there was enough room inside the piano that two little kids could sit quite comfortably. It was a hiding place that was used at least once during every hide-and-seek game. It wasn't long before I heard the familiar squeak of the lever as I was counting. I knew she was in there and I tip-toed quietly over to the piano, then pounded with both hands as hard as I could and on as many keys as I could cover. The trap door slid open and she came boiling out with her hands over her ears and threatening to kill me, but I had been smart enough to run behind Grandma as soon as I had pounded once.

It was Marian's turn to count, and my turn to hide. I knew that she wasn't smart enough to suspect that I would hide in the same spot. It was perfect. I crept into the piano as soon as she started counting and chuckled to myself at how clever I was. She would never think that I would be dumb enough to hide in there after what I had just done to her, and she would go down into the basement looking for me. I would then slip out and run to the base and be "home free." Just at that moment my eardrums imploded and a blinding, noise was vibrating my entire body. I grabbed the sliding door to escape but she was holding the lever on the outside. She continued to pound on the keyboard for what seemed like hours while I held my hands over my ears in a vain attempt to protect my shredded eardrums and tried to make my opinion heard over the din. Grandma finally came to the rescue and told Marian to stop wrecking the piano. I crawled out and began plotting my revenge.

Grandma had mouse traps around the house most of the time that had to be emptied every once in awhile. It was while I was emptying one that a wonderful idea struck me. It would take some planning and foresight but I was sure I could do it.

I set two of the traps and got a chair to stand on, placing the traps on the top of the piano just a couple inches from the edge so that they couldn't be seen from the floor. Then I waited for my chance.

A few days later Marian was doing her homework and I ran up, stole her pencil and tossed it up on the top of the piano. The piano was tall enough that Marian had to reach up and feel around on the top to find her pencil. She found the traps. I was laughing so hard I couldn't run away and wound up with a trap on each ear. I thought that was unfair, so I started plotting my revenge.

In the basement of Grandma's house were two bedrooms, one for the girls and one for the boys. Each room had a closet and the two closets were back to back with only a sheet of fiber board between them. In that fiber board was a hole about four inches in diameter. If I crawled into the boy's closet I could reach through the hole and touch the clothes hanging in the girls' closet.

Marian was deathly afraid of monsters and vampires and could be counted on for a ear piercing scream if you grabbed her leg from under the stairs or hid under her bed and made lip smacking noises in the dark, so one night I saw my chance. We had been telling ghost stories before bed so I knew she would be alert and not sleeping when the lights were turned off. I snuck over to the closet and crawled in. Reaching through the hole I shook her clothes just enough to get a response from her.

"WHAZAT?" came a hoarse squeak.

I waited. In my mind's eye I could see her sitting up in bed with the covers around her chin.

I shook the clothes a little bit harder and made a ghostly "WOOOOOO!"

Marian screamed, "Smarten up, Travis or I'll drop you!"

I shook the clothes. "I'm nooot Traaaviiiis. I juuust aaaaate hiiiim and I'll eat yooouu tooooo!"

She gave the proper response by screaming and hiding under the covers. I quickly ran out of the bedroom and around beside her bedroom door.

In Grandma's basement there was no ceiling, just the exposed floor joists and the upstairs floor on top of them. The bedroom walls in the basement went up to the floor joists and stopped, leaving room for a small boy to crawl over the wall between the floor joists and drop right down onto Marian's bed. I was just such a small boy.

I got a couple boxes to climb on and over the wall I went, dropping onto Marian's head with a banshee-like yell.

The next thing I remember is her sitting on my chest, punching me in the face and crying as if it was her getting hurt. By the time I got away I had a black eye and a bloody nose, so I began plotting my revenge.

Every day there were chores to do, pigs to feed and cows to milk. Marian carried grain to the pigs by the barn in five gallon pails and would do bicep curls with them as if they were a set of bar bells. She said it made her muscles bigger. I said they looked like flab to me. She showed me again how big they were. I got back up and said no more about them. She went off to feed the pigs and I helped Jim milk the cows, or at least I stood and supervised Jim as he milked. It was dark before chores were done so I saw an opportunity and ran around to the far side of the barn and started to howl like a coyote.

"AAAROOOOOOOOH!"

Marian heard me and started to cry. It was a long way to the house and she could hear what she thought was a coyote close by, between her and the house.

I howled again. Jim told her to quit being a cry baby and just run to the house. She started crying again but started running toward the house. I howled again and just as she rounded the corner of the barn I jumped out in front of her with a yell.

She was still carrying a metal bucket in her hand. She bent the bucket.

When I regained consciousness I began plotting my revenge.

Uncle Jim and Uncle Ed had built a boat that we played with in the swimming hole. They took two 2x4 boards and shaped them to look like sleigh runners and then nailed a sheet of tin on the bottom. It was two feet wide and three feet long. It looked like a small stone boat but it floated, sort of. If you sat in it and paddled with your hands as hard as you could, you might get close enough to the far shore so that you could wade back to land when it sank. When you were out in the boat, it was very important to paddle hard and not sink, because the cows and pigs had the water stirred up all the time and if you sank you came out smelling like pig manure and your mother would make you have a bath for sure that week.

Marian had a white frilly dress that she wore on Sundays and she thought it made her look like a princess. Once Keith and I had her tied up and sitting in the boat, she did look like a damsel in distress, but she sounded more like the dragon than the princess. As we pushed her out into the pond we discovered what a wailing ship sounded like.

It was Grandpa's rope and Jim's boat and yet it was me who got the spanking. How unfair is that? So I began plotting my revenge.

Marian and I were hauling straw with a Minneapolis tractor and a wagon that had a flat deck on it. We drove out to the field and put a load of straw on the wagon. It was my turn to drive the tractor so I got on the tractor and Marian got on top of the load of straw. As I pulled into the hay yard I turned the tractor as sharp as I could, the rear tire of the tractor caught the corner of the hay wagon and flipped it up. The whole load of straw came off quicker than it took to read about it. The only problem was that Marian was underneath the straw. I pulled enough straw bales off of her to see that she was still alive but little enough to give me a head start. I took off running as fast as I could. Marian dug herself out of the straw and jumped onto the tractor determined to run me over. It was a good thing that she didn't know how to shift the gears very well because she didn't have it in high gear and I was able to make it across the field to the bush before she caught me. I could have been seriously hurt or even killed, so I started plotting my revenge.

I looked out the window one day and spotted Marian sitting on the big inner tube doing her homework. The inner tube was a huge affair out of an earth mover tire, about eight feet in diameter and about two feet high. It was soft enough that she was sunk into it as though she was sitting in a big beanbag chair. The tube was about six feet away from the house and Marian was sitting in it on the side facing the house. I simply had no choice but to take advantage of the situation. I opened the window that was directly above her and jumped over her head onto the tube on the far side.

It was absolutely spectacular, the way she shot out of the tube like she'd been shot out of a slingshot, with her arms and legs flailing wildly. She smacked the wall of the house about four feet off the ground and her books went straight up into the air.

I got one of the worst beatings she ever gave me, so I began plotting my revenge.

It surprised me when I learned that most people cannot remember most of their childhood, especially the first few years. I can remember very clearly taking one or two steps and then falling down, crawling a little way, standing up and taking a few more steps and then falling again. I would crawl over to Marian and grab her pant leg and say, "Hep me up, Aunty Marian." It was the year I was in grade seven, and Marian's friends were standing around watching.

Marian had given me strict instructions that I was to never call her Aunty Marian in public, so naturally every chance I had, I did. I had never discovered anything that would embarrass Marian more than to fall down in the hallway at school in front of her friends, twitch a little and call her for help.

"When we get home I'm going to pound you to a pulp, you moron," she hissed.

"Do you know him?" Marian's friends asked.

"Never saw him before in my life."

"Don't hurt me, Aunty Marian!" I would plead as she started kicking me.

It worked so well to embarrass her that way, and I used the method so often that my teacher became worried and phoned my mother.

"Have you ever had Travis checked for cerebral palsy? He seems to fall down in the hallway just walking to and from class."

Mum asked me about it and I had to come up with a plausible story about my 'weak knee.' The last thing I wanted was to look like an idiot. Marian moved to Cardston with Grandpa and Grandma when I was in grade eight or nine and I never did get even with her.

Uncle Joe

I heard Uncle Joe talking loudly to a man dressed in a summer suit on the road down to the Belly River, but never came on the scene 'til after they had separated.

"What a man!" said the old man by way of exclamation. "He introduced himself by wantin' to sell me a set of fish hooks. I told him I wasn't in the habit of buyin' fish hooks in the fall and I usually save time and money and bait by doin' my fishin' in the fish market.

"Then he wanted for to sell me a yellow necktie. Why, I have no more use for a yellow neck tie than a locomotive got for a sidesaddle. And I told him so.

"Then he come out with a bottle of ointment that he was willing to warrant would cure corns, destroy dyspepsy, antidote bad digestion, check disability, dispel low spirits, restore the stomach, curb dysentery, correct bad habits, stop nosebleeds, demolish wakefulness, generate energy, heal bad feelings, preserve eyesight, break up the chills, scatter malaria, annihilate the cough, quench the thirst, distinguish pimples and slay biles; in short eradicate all the diseases of mankind.

"I looked at the man in surprise and remarked firstly that his medicine had too many irons in the fire to do a good job of healing of any kind. Secondly, it was against my principle to buy remedy in advance of illness. Finally I told him I didn't had any money.

"What you think he wanted to do then? He tried to sell me a pocket book. The idea of wanting to sell a man a pocket book when he didn't had any money. If I hadn't got so excited and thought the matter over, I'd of devised that fellow to change his occupation. Why he'll not make a living at that job. In order to sell a man something, one must know what a man am in need of.

"Just like my father used to say when I displayed the anxiety of the prospect of the hair upon my face: 'Why, if a beard is all that's necessary, a billy goat could run for office.'"

*F*rogs

Two young frogs from highland bogs
Had spent the night in drinking.
When morning broke and they awoke
And while their eyes were blinking,
A farmer's pail came to the swale
And caught them quick as winking
And then before they could make sense
And offer prayer for past offence
Old Farmer Gray that guileless man
Had dumped them in the milkman's can.

The can filled up and cover down
And soon they started off for town.
The luckless frogs began to quake
And shiver down in cold milk shake.
They quickly found their breath would stop
Unless they swim up on the top.
They kick for life, they fight and swim
Until their weary eyes grew dim.
Their muscles ached, their breath grew short.

Then gasping spoke one weary sport,
"Well, dear old boy, it's pretty tough
To die so young but I've had enough
Of kicks for life. I'll no more try it.
I wasn't raised on a milk diet."
"Tut tut!" the other fellow cried,
"A frog's not dead until he's died.
Keep on kicking, that's my plan.
We yet may see outside this can."

"It's just no use," faint heart replied,
Turned up his toes and gently died.
The braver frog undaunted still,
Kept kicking with a right good will
Until with joy too great too utter
Found he'd churned a lump of butter.
So climbing on this chunk of grease
He floated round with perfect ease.

Cowboy Poetry

If you're looking for culture and wisdom and wit,
Cowboy poetry is certainly not it.
They call these guys poets? Well now there's a joke.
And their poetic licence? It should be revoked.
Bunch of wanna-be-literates, chewin' their snoose
With the class of a goat and I.Q. of a moose.
Grade five education though you wouldn't know it.
They make two words rhyme and they think they're a poet.

They have no conception of rhythm or time.
With lines just like this one in order to get the rhyme.
The only culture they have is bacterial in form
And lives in their shorts where it's kept moist and warm.
They wear a big moustache to hide what's beneath
Like a wad of tobacco and two or three teeth.
They give themselves nicknames like Texas and Slim.
They think they're so funny but their wit's pretty dim.

I doubt if these guys will get published at all.
You can read it for free on a restroom wall.
'Makes his living by wit', which I doubt can be done
But I guess half a living is better than none.

Now writing a poem is no easy task
When all of your talent's in a 16 ounce flask.
He gets some lame joke that everyone's heard
Or maybe at best some quaint play on words.
Then he'll get himself sloshed, then he'll begin it.
See, the mind is much clearer when there's nothing in it.
The poet, he stands unashamed on the stage
With his most profound thoughts written down on one page.
He thinks they're enjoying his wisdom and wit
But what kind of fool writes a song about spit?
I've heard songs about horses and songs about dogs,
Manure on your boots and warts on a hog.
It's obvious why they have horses for friends,
'Cause that's where the scope of their intellect ends.

Wordsworth and Shakespeare, Longfellow and Poe -
These are the masters our children should know.
Is this your opinion? If so, well just shove it.
Cowboy poetry's the best and I love it.

How to Wear Out a Washing Machine

Starting when I was four or five, I remember riding with my dad on the tractor. I would stare out the back of the tractor cab at the cultivator plowing through the dirt. I was mesmerized by the stubble being turned over and fascinated by how the soft dirt would continually polish the hardened steel sweeps until they literally vanished. Each time the cultivator was lifted out of the ground I could see that the sweeps had a little more worn away. A set of cultivator sweeps would last for a couple hundred hours of being pulled through the dirt before they would be worn right off. I watched as discs, seed drills and other equipment wore out the same way. You have to realize that we had no Nintendo or television, so this was the next best source of entertainment for a kid like me.

As a result, I spent countless hours on the tractor watching the cultivator and other equipment wear out. I watched the wear on the tractor tires and even the spot of paint on the fender where Dad's hand rested and wore the paint away to leave the shiny silver metal exposed. It was fascinating to me how something soft could wear away something so hard over time.

In the sand box this same fascination influenced how I played. I had a rusty iron hook that was once part of a logger's cant hook. I would pull it through the sand like a cultivator shank, watching the sand polish the rust off the hook. Sometimes it would take a hour or so of diligent effort, pulling it back and forth through the sand to get it to shine.

One day, though, I lost the hook and was devastated by the loss of so precious a toy. I reported this loss to my mother, confident that her self-sacrificing generosity would not let me go toyless for too long.
She said, "Go play with a stick."

I soon found myself a stick with a short root still attached. This worked even better for my purposes, as I would drag the stick through the sand with the root acting as the cultivator sweep. The root wore out even faster than the steel did. So with concentrated effort, I discovered I could wear out three or four sticks a day and still get the same level of thrill as I did riding on the tractor.

But alas, one cannot spend one's entire life rubbing sticks in the sand, as much as one would want to. So naturally, I had to drag my sticks attached to a rope behind my bike. This would allow me to do my chores and other boyhood activities and still be able to wear out my quota of sticks.

My brothers soon discovered how much fun it was to drag sticks and how enthralling it was to see how, in just a matter of a few hours, an ordinary stick would go from coarse and rough to smooth and polished and eventually disappear. As sticks became scarcer, my brothers and I graduated to handmade wooden boats and other toys we deemed expendable. One day we built a wooden ship out of a two foot long 2x4 complete with guard rails, decks, mounted guns and smokestacks. The whole thing weighed several pounds. After dragging this boat up and down the driveway on our bikes for a couple hours we came to the conclusion that we needed more horsepower. Two hours of hard sweat and labor had only managed to rip off one smokestack and virtually no other wear could be seen. So we talked Mum into letting us drag it behind the pick-up truck as we made the ten mile trip up to the post office. It was wonderful. The three of us boys, Heathen Nathan and myself, were kneeling up side by side gazing over the tailgate as our boat disintegrated on the gravel road.

We couldn't wait to try other objects and soon nearly every trip to town we were dragging something – chunks of firewood, tires, steel gears, basically anything Mum would allow.

Quite often it would take several trips to town before whatever it was we were dragging wore out, but sometimes the rope or chain we used would wear out first or come untied and whatever it was we were dragging would go spinning off into the bush, depriving us of the thrill of watching it wear out.

When I got my driver's license it was a real dilemma between being able to drive and kneeling at the tailgate watching a tree branch wear out. Having a license did let me make more trips to town, though, to parties, youth activities, etc. and eventually to a job, thus enable me to wear out all kind of things. I always had something tied to my back bumper dragging along behind.

One day I had found an old dog leash with a collar and was dragging it down the highway when a gray haired old lady flagged me down. Before I could explain what I was doing she yelled at me and cursed me and swore she was going to report me to the SPCA. She refused to believe me that there was never a dog in the collar, and then she called my sanity into question when I swore I was trying to compare the wear qualities of leather and plastic dog collars. I tell you, some people are real loonies.

On most of our trips to Cherry Grove we would take the back road to avoid unnecessary traffic. The back road was very narrow and wound through, and over a set of very small but very steep hills. The road went over two of these hills in the course of about half a mile. They were about fifty feet high but less than two hundred yards from the bottom of one hill to the bottom of the other.

If a boy had the right passengers with him, he could get the front wheels of a vehicle airborne at the crest of either of these hills, giving his passengers a butterfly rush in their stomachs. You may ask, "So what? Who cares about some stupid hills?"

Well, just don't be impatient. Shut up and read on and you'll find out.

I'm seventeen years old at this point of the story. I invited all of my friends down to our place for a party.

That afternoon it was yard clean up day. My family spent the whole day cleaning the yard, sheds, and basement. We hauled all the garbage out and threw it in the only vehicle Mum said was worthy of such junk, my black truck.

One of the pieces of junk we hauled to the truck was an old washing machine. It was an old plunger type, consisting of an enameled steel tub on four legs. The antique monstrosity weighed about two hundred pounds. It wasn't one of those tin boxes that you buy nowadays; it was solid steel and built to last a lifetime. It probably would have lasted a lifetime if Mum hadn't used it for washing carrots and other vegetables instead of clothes. The three upside down bowl shaped plungers were too hard on clothing but the carrots that came straight out of the garden and into the machine in fifty pound batches, covered in sand and dirt, came out clean and peeled, ready for the freezer. The years of washing garden produce and pumping sand and grit had finally taken their toll on the poor old machine and now it was destined for the dump.

When the truck was loaded, my brothers jumped in and away we went, but the instant we were out of sight of the house, we stopped. Mum was usually very accommodating with our requests to drag something behind the truck but we knew that she had limits, which she always termed "common sense". We knew that if we wanted to wear out a washing machine, we had to do it without the restrictions of her "common sense." I am convinced that "common sense" has stifled many a creative genius.

The washing machine was promptly unloaded and tied to the back of the truck with a short length of rope. There was too much garbage in the back of the truck for anybody to ride back there, so we had to be content with the occasional glimpses that we had in the mirror as it bounced and rolled from the ditch on one side of the road to the ditch on the other. What a dust it stirred, too! The enamel was amazingly resilient and was slow to come off.

I had a hard time driving straight with my eyes glued to the mirror and when we came to the curves and hills on the back road I had to relax my vigilance, break my concentration and pay attention to driving for a minute.

Once we were past the hills it was several miles before we realized that the washing machine was no longer trailing us. We immediately stopped and after a minute or so of discussion, we decided that we would tie an old leather boot on in its place. Away we went again with the boot stirring up dust behind us.

We arrived at the dump, unloaded our load of garbage and spent five or ten or forty minutes sorting through all the unbelievably good stuff other people had thrown away. When we had it all loaded up we headed for home by way of the post office in Cherry Grove and then took the main road south.

We arrived home and Mum asked if we had trouble. It was pretty funny – Mum had thought the load we had brought home was the same load we had left with and that we had not made it to the dump. How silly can you be? We told her we had unloaded all that we had left with. She then gave us the same speech we had heard the last time we went to the dump, the one about being "a pointless exercise to go to the dump if we came home with more than we left with."

There was some discussion about hauling it all back, in which we all participated in as loudly as possible. Unfortunately we did not live in a democracy, so all our treasures were to be sent back where they came from on the next trip to town. That only gave us a day or so to smuggle some of the more valued pieces out of the truck and into one of the several hiding places we had for just such an emergency.

All my friends started arriving for the party soon after suppertime. We were planning on playing run-sheep-run down in the river valley but not everyone was there yet. Someone had forgotten to pick up Laurel and give her a ride down to our house. Steve volunteered to drive back to Cherry Grove and get her. If he took the back road and drove like mad he could be back in twenty minutes. We told him the rest of us would wait, so he jumped in his truck and took off.

We knew Steve was probably glad to spend some time alone with Laurel. I'm sure he wanted to invite her to go skunk hunting at the dump next time we went but hadn't as of yet had the nerve to ask her. The rest of us waited around the yard and twenty minutes turned into forty, then into an hour. It was just getting dark when they finally showed up and there was something definitely wrong with Steve's truck. Firstly, it sounded like a Sherman tank and secondly, the right front wheel was doing it's best to pull the truck towards the ditch, then it would change its mind and try for the other ditch.

There had been some change in Steve's mood too. My first thought was that Laurel had turned down his romantic date proposal.

When his truck stopped in the grass just off the driveway, Steve got out waving his arms and screaming. It seems that some "flippin' moron" left a washing machine dead-center in the road just over the crest of Butterfly Hill. He went on to explain how a steel washing machine lodged under a truck between the front axle and the oil pan limits one's ability to steer, and when one's only wheel with a functioning brake is six inches off the ground, stopping before the bottom of the hill was just as unlikely as Laurel wanting to go skunk hunting.

Steve and his truck rode the washing machine to the bottom of the hill where the road turned. When they hit the ditch, the washing machine wasn't able to negotiate the heavy willows and stopped, but it was able to hang onto Steve's tie rod and exhaust system and remove them with an efficiency seldom seen in modern conveniences.

It also gave Steve the proper angle of trajectory to clear the willows and land in a hay field.

He probably flattened some of the farmer's hay getting back to the road. I didn't ask.

Steve just couldn't get over it.

"What kind of a retard would leave a washing machine in the middle of the road?"

None of us knew and we told him so.

The next day we went and looked at the washing machine. It didn't appear to be damaged as badly as Steve's truck. My only question was, why can't they build appliances of that quality nowadays?

Alfred's Truck

*W*e had a lot more fun when Eric drove Alfred's truck than when Alfred drove it. Alfred was always too careful. I don't mean to say that we liked to ride with Eric. We just liked to watch Eric drive it. For instance, one time we were all trying to drive our 4x4's up Stonehocker's Hill in the snow. Eric was able to get Alfred's two wheel drive truck higher than any of the 4x4's. It was exhilarating to watch someone who disdainfully ignored the laws of engineering and relied exclusively on the laws of momentum and trajectory. It probably would have been just as much fun to watch him coming down the hill, but we missed it. We were somewhat preoccupied with getting out of his way.

One day Eric drove Alfred's truck to the church and parked it in the parking lot facing the church. We immediately set to work on preparations for the evening's entertainment by taking a couple of small hydraulic jacks and jacking up the rear axle of Alfred's truck so that the tires were about a quarter of an inch off the concrete. To the casual observer, and Eric was most definitely casual, the truck appeared to be sitting on the concrete as usual. By the time Eric was ready to leave almost everyone, except him, knew of the up coming show, and so they were prepared. There were quite a few people standing around in the parking lot casually observing.

Eric got in the truck and tried to leave.

With the axle jacked up, the wheels gently turned in the air. Eric naturally assumed that there was something wrong with the transmission so he followed the only logical course of action. He stomped on the gas pedal as hard as he could. When the speedometer was registering 80 mph and the truck wasn't moving, Eric changed his mind and put the transmission into park. This produced a very interesting series of noises which further confirmed in Eric's mind his first diagnosis of transmission trouble. Eric got out to see if he could see what the trouble was. As he looked under the truck he discovered the two jacks that were holding his truck up.

Of course, we were all standing around having thoroughly enjoyed the first act when he began making disparaging remarks about our sense of humor.

When he had first tried to leave an interesting thing had happened to his back wheels, which we pointed out to him. As the tires spun faster and faster the centrifugal force had expanded the tire's diameter. When the tires were motionless, they were a quarter of an inch off the concrete, but at 80 mph they had expanded enough to leave a black patch of rubber on the concrete. Eric made the next logical conclusion by himself. Getting the truck off the jacks was simply a matter of using centrifugal force to expand the tires enough to lift the truck and roll it off the jacks.

Eric got back in the truck to test his theory. We backed off a safe distance to watch. At 80 mph the tires began to touch the concrete. At 90 mph, they began to howl and smoke. When the speedometer read 105 mph the truck 'rolled' off the jacks. As the full weight of the truck came down on the wheels, they bit into the concrete with full traction and shot the truck over the sidewalk like a rocket sled on wheels, straight toward the side of the church. It was only because of his lighting reflexes and quick thinking that he was able to steer between the chokecherry bush and the corner of the building, missing both by a matter of inches. He shot straight over the church lawn, down the hill and across the ball diamond without slacking off on the gas. He was able to make his escape out of sight around the corner just before the bishop came out asking what the noise was all about and asking pointed questions about the two ruts across the church lawn.

Those who were inside the church watching out the window as he shot towards them later said that he was doing an excellent impression of a bug-eyed trout trying to display it's tonsils. If you promise to never tell Alfred, I won't either.

*B*ender and *B*rown

    *A*ny man who will go 'round behind your face and talk in front of your back about somtinks was a svindler. I heard Brown say veek before next 'bout me that I was henspecked husband. That was a lie. The proof of the eatin' was in the puddin'.

    I bin married forty years and still already I was not yet bullheaded. I still not live unter some petticoat government. Still I think it better a man insult mit his vife and get her device about somtink or other.

    These American vimmens never know notinks about his husband's business, when heart time comes and not much money, that don't make some difference mit her. Still she must have one full front dress petticoats mit every kinds trimming. Then that husband is bankrupt all to pieces. They call for the doctor and when the doctor comes that poor man dies. Then that voman was obliged to married mit another man who maybe she don't much like mit his four or six children on account of his other vife already and one or tree mother-by-laws, one second handed and the other a stepmother outlaw.

    Now a German goes dead it don't make some difference mit no one. No one would know it only maybe himself. His vife goes mit the business like notink should happen to sombodies.

    This same Brown went with me in the butcher business together. He was an American man. So was his vife. So many times this voman comes to his husband and says me must have money. Then she goes riding with her Ford car and her cardinal stripe stockings.

    One night me and my vife has a little talk about somtinks and next day I says to Brown, Brown my vife works in the store and cuts sausages and my daughter vorks in the store and cuts sauerkraut. Now your vife must work in the store and cut beef steaks or ve no more divide our profits equal.

Brown goes home and tells that about his vife. Next day she comes mit Brown around and we all have a little misunderstanding, everybody take part even my little dog Kaiser. Then the policemans comes along and arrests us for insulting the batteries or somtinks. Then the firm of Bender and Brown is broke up.

I goes mit my business and Brown goes mit his business. My income is more than my outcome but Brown goes around with his hands in his pockets and not a cent on his back.

Chewin' Gum

Once I met a pretty girl
I thought I'd like her some.
The only fault I had with her -
She's fond of chewin' gum.

Fond of chewin' gum,
fond of chewin' gum.
The only fault I had with her -
She's fond of chewin' gum.

Took her to the dance one night,
I thought we'd have some fun.
Right in the middle of a pleasant waltz
She stopped to chew her gum.

Stopped to chew her gum,
stopped to chew her gum.
Right in the middle of a pleasant waltz
She stopped to chew her gum

Introduced her to a friend,
I thought she'd like him some.
She didn't say a single word,
Just stood and chewed her gum.

Stood and chewed her gum,
stood and chewed her gum.
She didn't say a single word,
Just stood and chewed her gum.

I proposed and she accepted.
The wedding day had come.
The preacher was there to tie the knot
And she was chewin' gum.

She was chewin' gum,
she was chewin' gum.
The preacher was there to tie the knot
And she was chewin' gum.

I looked at her and I was disgusted
And there I turned and run.
Swore I'd never marry a girl
Who's fond of chewin' gum.

Fond of chewin' gum,
Fond of chewin' gum.
Swore I'd never marry a girl
Who's fond of chewin' gum.

Crushed

    Everyone sometime in their life will be afflicted by what is known as having a crush on someone. This is a terrible affliction that affects every young person at least once in their lives. The symptoms of the ailment are universal: a perfectly healthy and otherwise normal young person will spot someone of the opposite sex and will begin to develop heart palpitations, sweaty palms and severely reduced speech capabilities.

    If you are infected with this malady you will think nothing is wrong with you. In fact, the first symptom is an intense euphoria when in close proximity to the object of your desire. But when you walk up to say hello, you open your mouth, your brain falls out and you trip over it, severely bruising your ego and shattering your pride and dignity. At least that's how it happened to me.

    Jackie was the most exquisite creature I'd ever seen. She had a pretty, round face with the cutest dimples ever to grace feminine cheeks. I spotted her walking down the hallway in the high school and quit breathing. I sat down with my back to the wall, put my head between my knees and sat there until she had walked by.

    The high school had a large open area in the center of the school called the Agora. Students congregated there for meetings, rallies and to eat their lunches. Above the Agora was a suspended library where one could sit and look through the railing down into the Agora at the activities going on there, or one could sit and stare at Jackie eating her lunch or sitting with her friends at break times without being observed (if one chose to do so). I chose to do so.

    Actually speaking to Jackie was out of the question. I was short, scrawny and had a big nose. These liabilities effectively eliminated me from being a contender for her affections. So I was content to sit and stare at her and fill my daydreams with thoughts of talking to her.

In math class I sat and imagined myself walking up to her and saying, "Hi, Jackie. How are you?"

She would look me straight in the eye and say "Oh. Hi, Travis. How are you?"

Whereupon I would say something witty and she would laugh heartily and we would sit and eat our lunch together in the Agora where everyone could see us together and she would not be ashamed of me and my hands wouldn't be sweaty and my voice wouldn't crack and it would be just pure bliss. I would then gaze into her eyes and ask her for a date. She would look smilingly up at me and say…

"Travis, what is the sum of the problem we have been working on? Travis?....TRAVIS!!" The math teacher was yelling at me.

My mind came back to math class with a jolt.

"Dimples?"

I prowled around the hallways of the school trying to catch a glimpse of her during the breaks. I eventually figured out what her class schedule was and would make a point of timing my walks down the hallway in such a way that I would meet her somewhere every break. My heart would almost stop as she walked toward me and my knees went weak but I maintained my balance, nonchalantly walked by and then made a run for it to get to class on time.

It was pretty tough sometimes. I would have to run like a mad man to get my own books and then run to the far end of the school where her classes were in time to meet her going to her locker, and then hightail it back to my end of the school in time for my classes to begin. She never once looked at me when we met. She had no idea that I existed or that I was staring at her as I walked toward her or that I occasionally walked into the water fountain with my head turned around staring at her after she had walked by. With only ten minutes of frantic running through a half mile of hallway I was able to see her three or four times a day.

During lunch hour I made a point of sitting across the Agora from her so I could gaze uninterrupted for as long as twenty minutes at a time.

Such were my days spent, and my dreams at night were filled with visions of her dimpled cheeks and pretty smile.

One day in the middle of winter we had to get a tractor from Grandpa's place to our home. The problem was that the tractor had no cab. Mum said if I got off the bus at Grandpa's I could just bundle up and drive the tractor home. She asked me to stop at the store in Cherry Grove to get the mail and buy a bag of flour.

The day came and I got off the bus at Grandpa's. It was twelve miles home and the weather was about – 20 degrees so I put on two sweaters and a big plaid jacket, then a pair of Dad's bib overalls over top. On my head I had a red hardhat liner and a purple scarf. A huge pair of mitts completed the ensemble.

I headed out on the tractor toward home and before I got very far, I discovered that the earflaps on my hardhat liner weren't going to keep my ears warm. I stopped and crossed the scarf under my chin, then tied the knot on top of my head so the scarf added an extra layer over my ears. The ends of the scarf came out of the knot at right angles and froze in the wind so it looked as though I had two purple, tasseled donkey ears sticking out of the top of my head.

I stopped the tractor at the store and went in to get the mail and bag of flour that Mum had ordered. Helen, who ran the store, commented on my unique attire, and other people who were in the store had a little chuckle too. I was in no mood to argue so I put the bag of flour on my shoulder and walked out the door.

I stopped short. Jackie was getting out of her father's car, parked at the gas pump in front of the store. She hadn't seen me yet so I did the only thing I could think of. I grabbed the bag of flour and held it in front of my face.

This was not a particularly good idea, seeing as how I had three steps to go down to the ground. My feet never touched any of them. I landed splat on the ground on my face right at Jackie's feet. The bag of flour burst open and covered her legs and my face and head with flour. It nearly knocked the wind out of me and I choked for a few seconds in a cloud of flour.

There I was on my hands and knees, covered in flour and hacking and coughing, looking and sounding like a great asthmatic yeti with fuzzy purple donkey ears worshiping at the feet of some flour covered idol. I got up and ran for the tractor. I tried to get on but my baggy overalls hooked on the fender of the tractor and I was jerked back, flopping onto the ground on my back. I got up again and tried to get on the tractor, but once again the overalls hooked. This time I was so mad and frustrated that I heaved upward and the overalls ripped right down the side. I wasn't looking to see if she was watching but I'm sure I would have been watching if I had been in her place.

I tore off down the road on the tractor with my torn overalls streaming out behind in the wind like the grease stained cape of a superhero leaving the scene of the rescue. I did not feel much like a superhero and I was so embarrassed that I never felt the cold for the entire hour it took to get home.

For days I did not see her at school. I spent my time slinking around in the corners like a mouse in a cat house, afraid that if she spotted me she would broadcast the entire flour incident to the school and I would never be able to show my face in public again.

Not too many days later I was walking down the hall and didn't see her coming. Before I could duck into a doorway or stick a paper bag over my head she was right in front of me. As we met, she glanced up at me and then continued her conversation with her friends. Could it be that she didn't recognize me as the flour boy? I couldn't believe my good fortune, I must have been too covered in flour to be recognizable. But I wasn't sure that she wouldn't recognize me if she had more than a cursory glance at my face.

I resumed my prowling the hallways to obtain a few fleeting gawks at her.

About a month later at a church youth activity, my cousin Cara came in with a friend. I nearly died when I realized that the friend was in fact Jackie. During the course of the evening one of my female cousins caught me looking at Jackie and without even asking my permission, introduced me to her.

"Hi," said Jackie.

I looked at her sparkling blue eyes and my brain fell out.

"You've got eyes," I stuttered

"What?"

"I… uh… I said you forgot ice," I stammered, "for your drink."

"I prefer my hot chocolate without ice, thank you."

"Amazing! So do I," I said as I tried to get my brain back into gear.

Could it be that she really doesn't recognize me from the store? I had to find out for sure.

"Do you like flour?"

"Yes, I love flowers," she said with a smile. "What's your favorite kind?

"White," I said

"Oh. Really? Why white?"

"Better bread."

"What?"

"Ya. Brown makes the bread too crumbly," I declared.

She said she had to go find Cara and she walked away but she did turn back and look at me with a smile and a quizzical look.

A few minutes later Cara and Jackie returned. We talked for awhile. With Cara there, Jackie didn't seem so intimidating, and during the conversation I actually made her laugh out loud at a story I was telling. But then she asked me if I would like to dance. My brain fell out again and I said yes.

What was I thinking? I had a hard enough time walking when she was close and now I would have to dance? I stumbled out onto the floor, praying that it would be a fast song where we could stand a few feet apart and just twitch and jerk for awhile the way kids my age danced. But it was not to be. They started playing a slow waltz. Jackie stepped up and took hold of my hand. I don't know how it got there but my other hand was around her and touching the small of her back. My heart quit beating again and the sweat started running down the back of my neck into my underwear.

I had never been so thrilled or so terrified in my life. She was smiling and laughing not even making jokes about my big nose.

"Would you like to go out with me on Friday?"

I had no time to think about it, the words had just leapt out on their own and it was too late to stop them. I had just started to apologize when I realized she had said yes.

The rest of the night is a blur. She danced with me several more times and then she and Cara had to go.

"See ya tomorrow," she called as they left.

I went out and sat in the snow in front of the church, staring at the stars until the bishop came and told me to go home before I froze to death.

The next day at school I was walking into the Agora to eat my lunch when I heard my name called. It was Jackie. She was sitting with some of her friends and she was beckoning me to come and sit with them. She slid over, giving me room to sit beside her.

I was so engrossed in being so close to her that I can't even remember what I had for lunch that day, but I can remember what she smelled like. It was like sitting in the field of flowers in the movie Wizard of Oz, where the scent goes straight to your mind and shuts it off. I spent the next two days in such a state of bliss that even the strictest teachers gave up and let me stare at the wall in my own world of thoughts and fantasy.

Friday came. I talked to her and we agreed to meet at a certain place at a certain time. I rushed through my chores and gobbled my supper. I had a shower and brushed my teeth, even though it was only Friday, and came into the kitchen to ask Mum if I could borrow the truck.

"What for?" she asked.

I couldn't very well tell her I had a date with a girl. Not with Heathen Nathan and Shelby sitting right there waiting for any ammunition to harass me with. If that kind of information got to my uncles and aunts they would torment me forever, and admitting to your mother that you liked a girl and had a date would open up a whole can of worms and birds and bees that I wasn't prepared to deal with.

"I was invited to go to an activity."

It wasn't the whole truth but it wasn't a lie either. I hoped it would be enough.

"No. You went to a party once already this week."

I pleaded and begged and made promises I intended to keep. I did everything I could think of except telling her I had a date, but it was no use. Mum would not let me use the truck. I couldn't take my own truck either, because firstly, I wanted to impress her and secondly, I wanted to get her to and from home in one piece. The chance of doing either in my truck was nil.

I went to my room with my world crashing down around me. How could I face her if I stood her up?

I would have to call her. I ran back downstairs and into the kitchen to use the phone. Heathen Nathan were both there playing a game. I waited for them to leave so I could make my call in private. They just sat there playing their stupid game and acting like they didn't know that I was fighting for the very existence of my future happiness.

I tapped my foot and drummed my fingers on the table hoping they would get the hint and leave.

"What's the matter, Trav?" Nathan asked.

"SHUT UP!! Who said anything about a date!?" I yelled at him.

I couldn't think straight. What was I to do? How could I ever face her again if I stood her up? I couldn't. It was that simple.

The only choice I had then was to run off and join a monastery, vowing a life of celibacy and humiliation. The only reason I didn't was the fact I would need the truck to get to the nearest monastery, and if I had the use of the truck I would have no use for the monastery.

I couldn't get up the nerve to phone her. How could I explain to a girl that her date's mommy wouldn't let him go?

The next day at school I hid in the darkest corners I could find and avoided anywhere she might be. It was several days before I saw her again and all I could manage was a mumbled "I'm sorry." I turned and ran before I had to listen to her scathing denunciation of my betrayal.

I never got up the courage to talk to her again, but I did buy a copy of the year book because I knew it would have a picture of her in it.

I knew then why it is called 'having a crush' on someone. I'd been crushed.

Living in the Cemetery

Uncle Ed had a business selling grave covers and headstones. He asked Kelly and me if we wanted to work for him that summer during the school holidays. The thoughts of getting away from the farm and having money of my own were enough to overcome my apprehensions of working for Ed. So I told him okay.

We were going to be gone for about five weeks so Kelly and I spent the day before packing all the clothes and bedding we would need. The morning we left, I packed all our gear out onto Ed's porch, ready for Kelly to load it into the pickup. Then I helped Ed load the big truck with gravel, cement bags, forms and other tools we'd need.

Ed got into the big truck and started off. Kelly and I jumped into Ed's Datsun pickup and followed him down the highway. We were headed into the Peace River area, stopping at almost every cemetery between Lac La Biche and Grande Prairie. We got to Lac La Biche, got out our tools and began work on the graves that Ed had contracted to do.

There was a gas powered cement mixer mounted on the back of the truck. It was my job to shovel sand and gravel from the back of the truck into the cement mixer. Then when the cement was ready, I would dump it into a wheelbarrow and bring it over to the grave. I dumped the cement into the form and Ed and Kelly would finish it with trowels. We worked in the hot sun, sweating and dusty all day, leveling the dirt on the graves and then shoveling gravel and cement and pouring it into the forms.

When evening came we were glad for a break and a rest.

"You guys set up the tent and I'll cook some supper," Ed said.

I dragged the tent out of the back of the truck and started to look for the poles to set it up with. It was at that point I realized that Kelly hadn't loaded any of our gear into the truck. He tried to blame me, but I distinctly remember hauling it out onto the porch. He should have realized that I was busy helping Uncle Ed and that the gear still needed to be loaded. The way they both carried on you would think it was a major catastrophe. We still had the tent. No poles or ropes for it, but if we spread it out flat and then folded it over once we could pretend it was a big, rough, smelly, uncomfortable sleeping bag.

I tell you, the two of them whined about it for the next month. Ed slept on the seat of his truck, Kelly slept rolled up in the tent and I slept on the ground wishing that I hadn't blamed Kelly for leaving the gear. We had no clothes, food, tent poles or cooking utensils. It was going to be a wonderful adventure, just like back in my old Boy Scout days.

Camping out in the open in graveyards leaves one open to odd looks from local people driving by. Some people would stop by and ask what we were doing when they saw our camp fire. In the cemetery in Kinuso, a local fellow stopped by and told us that the graveyard was haunted and that we shouldn't sleep there if we knew what was good for us. That night we sat around the fire talking about ghosts, zombies and all the other things that make for a restful sleep when one is planning on spending the night in a cemetery. I went to sleep lying on my back on top of a marble slab to stay out of the dewy grass.

In the middle of the night, when I was fast asleep, Kelly got up and stood at my feet and then holding himself rigid, fell forward over top of me and caught himself with his hands on each side of my head, stopping with his nose a quarter inch from mine. Of course I woke up when his hands slapped the slab by my ears. I opened my eyes and his face was right there. My screams woke up Ed who was in the truck fifty yards away. Kelly thought it was really funny but I didn't sleep for the rest of the night.

The next day, because I was so tired, I misjudged my footing and fell into the cement mixer. There I was head down in the cement mixer with my legs flailing around as it rolled me over and over, dumping cement on my head. Kelly and Ed did nothing but laugh at me. By the time I got out I was scraped up so bad I could hardly walk and they were still laughing. To top it off I had wet cement in my hair and down the back of my neck, and it had already been a week since I'd had a bath or had even taken my shoes off. There was no prospect of getting a bath for at least another week. I wasn't impressed with their attitude and lack of sympathy.

That night I was still covered with cement dust. My hair, which was almost collar length when clean, stuck out rock hard like a wire brush. Kelly hadn't bathed or showered either, so the two of us looked like ghouls in the daylight. In the dark it was worse, and in the bright moonlight Kelly was absolutely hideous. He gave me the same compliment.

We could hear a party going on just down the road from us and came up with a way to change our looks from being a liability to an advantage. We knew the local folklore about the graveyard being haunted so we stayed up listening to the music. When the party started to break up we hid behind some headstones. We were sure there had been some drinking at the party and we were counting on some alcohol induced enhancement of our intended display.

It was better than we had hoped. As vehicles drove by, we rose up out of the graves and ran toward the cars coming down the road. There were vehicles that hit the ditch and others that turned around in a cloud of dust, spinning wheels and screaming girls. I've been curious ever since if the rumors of haunting still persist.

When we got to Peace River we had been on the road for twenty one days and Ed was starting to complain about needing a bath. He decided that he would rent a hotel room for the night and we could bath and wash our clothes. My underarms were getting as crusty as buffalo chips, my dandruff consisted of concrete flakes and I wasn't sure if what I felt in my shoes was sand or ants.

We stopped at a motel and Ed went in and asked for a room. The manager looked at him and told him there was no way. Ed figured it might have something to do with the smell so he went down to the river and went for a swim. He found a shirt under the seat of his truck and he put it on, then went back to the same motel and asked for a room. The manager didn't recognize him and rented him a room.

I had a hard time getting my shoelaces undone because they were so full of concrete, but I finally got them loose. I took my shoes off and tried to peel my socks off but one of them broke. Ed took our clothes and went to wash them. He brought them back and I was surprised at the color of my sock and accused Ed of stealing someone else's sock but he claimed it was mine.

When Ed went to wash our clothes, Kelly and I stayed in the room in our underwear and watched professional wrestling on TV. We were laughing about how fakey the wrestlers on TV were and we started pretending we were wrestlers, pushing each other around and over-exaggerating the flops and falls that wrestlers make. Kelly picked me up in some goofy wrestling move and threw me on the bed. He looked up saw the manager outside, looking in through the window at us standing there in our underwear. Kelly quit wrestling, closed the curtains and then sat on the bed threatening me that if I told anybody he would kill me.

Don't tell him that you know.

In those days I could eat. I have never met anyone who could eat more. In fact I was so good at it that I could have gone pro but just never had the offer. I once won a bet for the rig crew I was working with. They had bet that their derrick man was a bigger pig than the other crew's derrick man. So the next morning in camp we settled the argument.

In order to prove my crew right, I wound up eating twenty six eggs, twenty six slices of bacon, twenty six sausages, twenty six slices of toast and a bunch of juice to wash it down. It didn't stay down but I had won. Come to think of it, there was some money that changed hands but I never got any of it and I'm the one who suffered all day.

Anyway, Ed knew that I could eat, and one day he made me an offer - if Kelly and I beat our record of graves covered in one day he would take us out to a restaurant for breakfast and I could eat all I wanted. The idea of breakfast that was something other than hotdogs and dry bread motivated us to work. We set a new record, finishing ten covers in one day.

The next morning he took us to a restaurant in Grimshaw and when the cute young waitress came to take our order we ordered the breakfast special. She brought it out and asked if there was anything else.

I said, "Yes. One more please."

By the time she brought the second one I was finished the first.

"Would you like anything else?"

"Yes. One more please."

She brought it.

"Would you like anything else?"

"Yes. One more please."

By that time she was looking at me kind of funny and it had become a contest of wills. Ed and Kelly were cheering me on and telling me that the more I ate the more impressed she'd be. She was very cute so I soldiered on through about six specials. I had reached my limit and had to quit when she asked if I would like dessert.

Ed said, "Sure. What kind of pie do you have?"

I shook my head trying to signal him to quit.

She listed off several varieties and Ed chose pumpkin.

She thought it was funny when she came back with an entire pumpkin pie with ice cream and set it in front of me.

The whole kitchen staff had come out to watch. Ed and Kelly told me that I couldn't let them down so I went to work on the pie. I did it, but an hour later I was violently ill and stayed that way for the rest of the day. We didn't set any new records.

Kelly and I went back to the restaurant the next day and asked the waitress and her friend if they would like to go to the drive-in movie with us. They said yes but we would have to wait until they were off shift. We were driving Ed's truck which was a piece of junk and didn't have enough room for four of us, so they said they would drive.

We made arrangements that they would follow us back to our camp so we could leave the truck there and tell Ed where we were going. They followed us down the road and when we pulled into the graveyard where we had been camped for several days, they could see Ed cooking his hot dog on a fire and our tent propped up with sticks and baler twine. They turned around at the approach into the cemetery and drove away, leaving us standing there wondering what the matter was.

Ed and Kelly didn't get along all the time for some reason. Ed hardly ever teased us and hardly ever gave us a hard time. Except when he was awake. Kelly liked to buy a bottle of pop that he would save for the afternoon when it was hot and he was very thirsty. He would spend all morning thinking about his pop until he could stand the thirst no more. Then he would walk over to the truck and look under the seat where he had left it only to discover that Ed had found it and had drunk it already. The next morning he would buy a bottle and hide it in the tool box, and in the afternoon when he could stand the thirst no more he would walk over to the tool box and discover that Ed had found it and drunk it already.

Each day he would hide it in a different spot and Ed would find it. There would be the same old fight and holler. Kelly was getting so mad he was ready to shoot Ed and Ed said he was very grateful for the all pop Kelly kept buying him.

One morning Kelly finally figured out how to keep Ed away from his pop. He bought a liter bottle of Sprite, took the top off and after making sure that Ed was watching, spit in it several times. He put the top back on and set it on the seat of the truck. Ed didn't say a word but just stood and watched. Kelly turned and started walking across the cemetery to where we were working. He was only twenty yards away when he looked back at Ed and was just in time to watch Ed drinking the last few drops of his pop.

Kelly liked his steak well done. It irritated me to no end to see someone ruin a perfectly good steak by burning it into an unrecognizable mass the way he liked it, and I told him so. He replied that anyone who ate their steak raw like I did was in danger of all sorts of disease. He was being very sarcastic, as I liked my steak cooked medium rare like any civilized person would. But he, being an uncivilized boor, wouldn't know a good steak if it bit him on the leg. As we discussed the matter, he claimed that eating a raw steak would kill you. I bet him that it wouldn't.

We went to a restaurant to settle the bet. We walked in and ordered our dinner. When the waitress asked us how we would like our steak done, Kelly told her that he would like his well done. I asked for mine raw.

"Do you mean very rare?" she asked me.

"No," I said, "stone cold raw."

She looked at me with a skeptically raised eyebrow and left.

She came back awhile later with Kelly's steak with all the trimmings and placed it carefully in front of him. She then brought out a plate and plunked it down in front of me unceremoniously. It had a raw steak on it all right, but the trimmings consisted of a raw unwashed potato and an unwashed raw carrot. Apparently she thought this was very funny.

I couldn't let her get away with that, so I grabbed the steak in one fist and the potato in the other and went to work eating them both as fast as I could. The waitress stood and watched for a minute and then left. A few seconds later the manager came to our table and invited us to leave.

He looked at Kelly. "We have paying customers who are losing their appetites. Will you please take your pet with you and leave?"

I never did get to prove that a person could eat a raw steak and live. Kelly said he would have killed me anyway even if the steak didn't.

We spent the summer traveling and sleeping in almost every cemetery in northern Alberta. There are many cemeteries in the north that still bring back fond memories. In fact, Helen says that I am the only person she knows who has fond, happy memories connected to cemeteries.

I have written many resumes when applying for jobs, but only once have I put down 'grave covering'. After having to explain what "living in a graveyard for the summer running a shovel" meant, I found it was easier to not put it on my list of previous job experiences.

*T*elephoning

Neighbours not too far from here
Put in a telephone last year.
Farmers put in a rural line
With instruments all fixed up fine.
All you had to do was ring,
Every phone went ting-a-ling -
Once for Simpson, two for Boggs,
A long and a short called for old Scroggs.

Every time a signal rang,
To the phone each farmer sprang,
Slyly grinning and softly took
The receiver from the hook.
He'd slap his leg at everyone.
Telephoning's lots of fun!
Somehow in a month or two,
Trouble dark began to brew.

Farmer Jones got boiling hot,
Heard Scroggs calling him a sot.
Farmer Scroggs got angry too,
Heard Smith telling what he knew.
Smith heard Johnson telling lies,
Paid him off with two black eyes.
Johnson heard young Issac Boggs
Under bidding him on hogs.
Boggs o'erheard a sneaking cur
Making love to his best girl.

Women too were in the muss,
Raised a most tremendous fuss.
Everyone from Scroggs to Jones
Were in glass houses throwing stones.

Now the line is over grown,
Wires rusted, poles o'erthrown.
Former friends are deadly foes.
They're all full of griefs and woes,
All too mad to speak a word
Because of things they'd overheard.

The Hero

The sun was already up when he climbed out of bed. He dressed quickly and slipped on his chaps, spurs and his hat that hung on the bed post. He buckled on the two pistols that were his trademark, tied low for easy reach. His hands streaked down and snatched them up faster that the eye could follow. He snapped off a couple imaginary shots at a mark on the wall. He smiled a smirking sneer that openly displayed his almost arrogant confidence in his ability.

After a hurried breakfast he strode outside to where his horse stood leaning against the corral fence.

His mahogany coloured stallion broke into a run as he leaped into the saddle. He loved the feeling of freedom the wind gave as it blew through his hair. He shouted encouragement to the stallion as he galloped as hard as he could go across the desert, not slackening the pace till he was sixty eight miles from the ranch house. The stallion wasn't sweating too hard, so he left him laying down in the grass while he scouted for sign of the stray herd he had tasked himself with finding.

The herd of steers had stampeded during the night but stopped in the canyons on the west end of the ranch.

For several miles down through the cactus and mesquite choked canyons, he tracked them on foot. At the foot of the mountains he finally found them virtually corralled in a natural box canyon. The mouth of the canyon was their only escape route.

He pulled out his hunting knife and cut down fifteen or twenty six-inch pine trees to build a temporary fence.

Just as he was finished the fence, a snapping twig alerted him to the fact that he was being stalked. It was old One Eye, the wounded mountain lion that had terrorized the local peasants.

The lion leaped. The battle was quick and brutal and he showed the lion no mercy, quickly dispatching him with his knife.

He ran back and picked up his horse and returned to begin branding.

With his unerring aim with a rope and his sure footed stallion, it was no time at all before the twelve hundred head herd was branded and headed for home.

He knew he was over a hundred miles from home so he would have to push the herd hard to be home before dark.

Home was where she was. The only woman in his life. He had never spent a night without her since they had first met and he swore he would not let tonight be the first.

He was within sight of the ranch house when it came. It must have been an Apache arrow that made him stumble, but the horse went down and he hit the ground hard. His eyes watered with the pain in his knee. He took a quick look – the Cheyenne arrow had ripped a horrendous gash across his knee. Blood poured from the gaping wound. He knew the end was near and the Sioux warriors would be closing in now.

Suddenly she was there beside him. She had heard the cries and was there for him. She cradled him in her arms and looked at his wounded knee and said in a comforting voice, "Don't worry, we'll wash it off and put a band aid on it. Come on, now, it's lunch time and you have to get ready for kindergarten this afternoon."

So she carried his horse in one hand and him in the other as they went back into the house.

These pages were intentionally left blank to increase the size of the book and thus give you the impression, when you bought it, that you were getting more for your money.

The following story was written by my daughter Kyla. It is included in this book just to humour her. Unlike my stories, Kyla has exaggerated many parts of this story and it shouldn't be believed. Besides that, everybody had fun even though they still deny it.

The Canoe Trip

Not so long ago, in a land not so far away, there lived a small but contented family. There was a father, a mother, a daughter, and a young son. The father loved camping and roughing it in The Great Outdoors. The rest of the family didn't mind camping as long as they stayed relatively dry for the most part of the outing.

One day the father announced that the family was going to go camping. The family agreed as the forecast said sun and clear sky for the next week.

As the family was packing up their gear for the jaunt, the father started talking about how wonderful it would be and how he loved to sit in a canoe and look up at the precipitous bank of a river. The family questioned the father on his remarks. It never had occurred to the mother, daughter and young son that the father had failed to announce the whereabouts of the camping trip. It turned out the father was planning a two day canoe trip down the river.

"But Father," said the young son, "we don't even have a canoe."

"Not to worry, my boy, for I have already considered that. We will take your grandfather's canoe, the same canoe that I rode in when I was a youngster," reassured the father.

The mother and daughter shared a worried glance.

"But dear," cautioned the mother, "that canoe is very old. Are you sure it is safe to take down the river?"

"Of course it is! Why, that boat never had a leak in it! Do you not trust me?" asked the father.

"Yes, my dear, we trust you. I just wanted to make sure," said the mother softly.

When the family was all packed and ready to go, they piled into their 4x4 and headed toward their grandfather's and grandmother's house to fetch the vessel that would carry them throughout their excursion. As they loaded it into the truck, the grandfather said to the father, "Careful, she leaks a bit, here and there."

"Dear!" the mother shrieked, "we cannot go in a leaky canoe for we shall all become wet."

"Father, I cannot go in a leaky canoe, for what if it sinks?! I am afraid of fish and as you know the river is full of enormous fish with vast amounts of enormous teeth!" cried the daughter.

"Father, I hate being wet, for whenever I am wet mother becomes angry!" wailed the young son.

"Mother, daughter, young son! That is enough of your whimpering! He said the canoe leaks here and there, not everywhere. I promise we won't get wet. Now let us get into our truck and proceed on our camping trip," commanded the father.

The family again piled into the 4x4, but this time advanced to the river. Along the way the father continued with his daydreaming about how pleasant and relaxing the outing would be. The mother, daughter and young son panicked.

When they arrived at the river's edge, it was edging lunch time. The father pointed out that there would be no time for eating as they had to get to the halfway point by sundown. The family unloaded the canoe and provisions that they would need out of the truck.

They wrapped everything – bedding, food and the tent – in large tarps.

"This is so things will stay dry if the canoe gets flipped over in the rapids," the father knowingly said.

As they boarded into the craft, the father proceeded on handing out the life jackets. The daughter and young son began to cry.

The mother tried to reassure them, and said that it was okay to wear antique things. The father stated that the life jackets the family were wearing probably were the same ones that the brave and noble Christopher Columbus used on his voyage to find America. This only made the daughter and young son cry harder.

The father sighed as he pushed the canoe out into the open water.

The gentle flow of the river pushed them along at a reasonable pace. Suddenly the young son let out an ear splitting scream.

"My feet are soaking wet!" he howled.

The entire family looked down at their feet and to the father's shock and amazement, the canoe had five inches of water in the bottom and it was still rising.

"I…I just don't understand it," stuttered the father.

The mother slowly calmed the daughter down and the daughter eventually let go of the hotdog stick that she was going to strike the father with.

"Well, what are we going to do dear?" questioned the mother. "You said it wasn't necessary to bring a bucket so we trusted you and didn't bring one."

"Now, now just wait…I'll think of something." The father thought for a moment. "I have it! Mother, you brought drinking glasses did you not? Young son, take one of the drinking glasses that mother brought and begin bailing."

So that is what the young son did for the rest of the trip, bailing like mad with a blue plastic drinking glass.

The father said, "Young son, if you kept your other thumb on the hole it wouldn't shoot water up into your eye so bad."

After they got the young son so he could bail and not get in anyone's way, the father thought that this would be a good time for the mother to learn how to paddle the canoe so when they arrived at a place with white water rapids that required paddling expertise, she would be prepared.

Just as the mother was getting to understand where to paddle to make it go where she wanted it to, the family and their leaky canoe rounded a bend in the river. Dead ahead of them were rapids. They weren't huge rapids that would crush any form of craft that passed over them. But if a person wanted to get through them in a boat, they would have to have some idea of what they were doing. This person was definitely not the mother.

The mother began to question the father's judgment, using words like Titanic and Davy Jones' Locker, and the father, having little to no patience for flustered women, began high decibel paddling instructions.

The boat tossed and tipped and all the while the mother and father shouted about what they were doing, and the daughter and young son again began to cry.

When the family thought that the end was nigh at hand, the rapids ceased and the river again gently flowed as it once did.

As they floated along the river, all of the members of the crew were having different feelings about what was happening to them. The mother was still somewhat upset about the father being angry at her for her incompetence, not to mention that her good kitchen drinking glass was being scratched up by the canoe floor. The daughter was cranky because she was soaking wet and the mosquitoes were biting at any piece of bare flesh she had. The young son was preoccupied with bailing that he didn't have time to think of much else. The father was relaxing and enjoying the cool breeze and gazing at the dark clouds that were beginning to form over his head.

As they drifted along in silence for an eternity of time, the daughter spoke up. "I think I just felt rain."

"Oh nonsense, it isn't supposed to rain and it won't."

Just as the father completed his encouraging annotations a thunderclap was heard throughout the entire party of drenched sailors.

"Dear, as much as I trust your judgment, I think that we should stop and make camp. It is going to be dark soon anyway and we are all hungry," commented the mother.

The father grumbled as he steered the canoe toward a nearby bank. The troop stepped out of the canoe and began to set up camp. As they took the large tarps out of the canoe, to their surprise the large tarps had enormous holes, and the water that had leaked in the boat had seeped into their gear destroying any food that wasn't in cans or plastic and had sodden all of their sleeping paraphernalia.

Just as the family thought that things couldn't get any worse, it started to rain. Not just a light sprinkle, an out-and-out pouring rain.

The family hurried and tried to set up the tent as fast as they could. The father had a brilliant idea of placing the tarp, which was still dripping wet, of course, under the tent to stop any further soaking of the tent floor by the wet sand. The rest of the family didn't agree with this and the mother later said, after the trip, that the father was probably suffering from hypothermia at the time.

But being obedient and all trusting in the father as the family was, they placed the tarp under the tent. Grabbing what little food that wasn't soaking wet, the family jumped into the tent.

As they sat and ate their dinner of cold spam and soda crackers, the young son noticed that again his feet were getting wet.

The family looked down. To the father's shock and amazement, the tent was filling up with water.

"I just don't understand," said the father.

The family growled at him and crawled into their cold, wet sleeping bags and pretended to go to sleep.

The next morning the family got up and waded to the tent door. They didn't wake up for they had never actually gone to sleep. Whatever wasn't even remotely dry before was definitely wet now. The mother, daughter, and young son decided to revolt against the father and have a mutiny. They told the father that they would have no more of this. The father, finally seeing the light, agreed. He knew that if the crew mutinied the captain would go down with the ship, and with the ship he had, that was very possible.

So the family once again packed up the canoe and started down the river. The young son was again kept busy bailing. They knew that the bridge, which marked the halfway point, was not far.

When they arrived at the bridge, the father walked to the nearest house and called some of their friends to come and pick them up before the mother, daughter and young son were guilty of a murder.

We all survived. I am the daughter of the father and mother, and the young son is my little brother. Dad says he is building an iron raft for our next trip. He may have to go alone.

*O*h *C*hristmas *T*ree

(Sung to the tune of Oh Christmas Tree)

Oh Christmas tree, oh Christmas tree.
A symbol so prophetic
Of children's greed and too much feed,
No wonder you're synthetic.
Synthetic leaves so shiny green,
You smell like polyethylene.
The ads prevail, we buy on sale
The trees that are synthetic.

Oh Christmas treats and Christmas eats -
That's why I'm diabetic.
The pills I take for Christmas' sake.
Whoops! that one's diuretic
Oh my synthetic Christmas tree,
With one pathetic gift for me .
Oh Christmas tree, oh Christmas tree.
I see why you're synthetic.

Milking The Dragon

    Heath drank milk. Not just a glass at breakfast and a little on his cereal. I mean that it was his hobby, what he did for relaxation and entertainment. You see, we had no television and Heath could think of nothing better to do.

    Nathan drank milk twice, once when he was born and then again once a couple of years ago when an unwitting hostess poured some milk on his porridge and he didn't want to appear rude. As a result Nathan is the only one who bears no guilt in the following record.

    Shelby never drank very much either but she never felt sorry for me, so she does share some of the guilt for the suffering I endured as a youth.

    Hayden drank milk because it came in single serving sized gallon jars which could be easily obtained from the fridge in the middle of the night when he got up.

    Mum made cheese and cottage cheese whenever there was enough milk to do it. She had two refrigerators in the kitchen, one for the eggs and the leftover potato from supper the night before, and one refrigerator dedicated strictly for milk.

    I had no hobbies. Neither did I have time for relaxation or recreation. All my waking hours were spent milking the cow to keep up with the demand. Between Heath, Hayden and Mum, the family milk consumption was just less than that of the Glenwood cheese factory. To make matters worse, our dairy (and I use the word very loosely) cows were usually some young Hereford heifer that had lost its calf. Judging from their temperament it wouldn't have surprised me to learn that the reason they had lost their calf was that they had eaten their own offspring.

    Dad would make the decision which cow would be milked that year sometime in the spring during calving season and make the announcement one morning.

"We'll need to catch number 32 this morning."

"Why?" I would ask nervously, hoping it was something as simple as calving difficulties. "Isn't she the one that jumped the fence last year and gored John's dog?"

"No that was number 33. Number 32 is the Charolais-cross cow. You know, the one where we had to hide in the bale feeder for an hour last year after we tagged her calf. I can't find her calf this morning and there is something wrong with her. She has blood all around her mouth."

Getting the cow in was simply a matter of letting her see you through the open gate of the corral. When she charged at me Dad would shut the gate behind her and I would run up the chute in front of her, leap nimbly over the side of the chute and stand shaking and trembling until the adrenalin rush was over.

"Why can't you do the running once?" I asked him.

"You don't have any kids to support."

That made no sense to me but I said nothing.

Once the cow was snubbed down to a good sturdy corral post with one leg tied back, she could be milked.

"Go ahead," said Dad. "You're younger than me. Don't be scared. Just get in there and milk her, she'll be fine."

Dad had a vicious sense of humor and would say, "We'll just give her a little grain each time we milk her and in a couple of days she'll stand for you."

He thought this was funny for two reasons: first, because we never had any grain to give her and secondly, because he would go off to work on the rigs the next day leaving me to do battle with the cow by myself.

Dad tried this once when we lived at the little house and I was only about four years old, so Mum tried to milk the heifer. Mum and I left the house and strode confidently out to the barn with the milk pail in hand and opened the barn door. The confidence that had accompanied us to the barn abandoned us right there. I don't recall the details of the event accurately enough to relate them, but in Mum's own words, "We got two squirts into the pail, and then we went back to the house. When Dad got home I just turned on the waterworks, and it worked so well he never asked me again."

I always wondered why my waterworks never worked on Mum the same way. She would drive me out in the morning to milk the cow regardless of weather or illness. Many was the time when I was at death's door, literally gasping for breath suffering from a chronic infirmity that I had on school days, and Mum would drive me mercilessly out into the cold to do battle with the dragon.

"For pity's sake," she'd holler. "If you don't get a move on you'll be late for the bus again."

The dragon was the vicious, bloodthirsty killer who waited in her stall in the barn silently plotting how best to disembowel me.

Now there are some things you need to know about our barn and the dragons that infested it. The only thing we had that could be called a barn was a hole in the side of a cut bank about sixteen feet wide, five and a half feet high and about thirty feet long. Dad had taken a Cat and pushed a dugout into the side of the cut bank, and then put a roof over it. The floor of the barn was horizontal for about fifteen feet and then sloped upwards till it met the roof at ground level at the back of the barn. If you were standing on the ground at the back of the barn it looked like a pile of lumber had been thrown on the ground at the edge of the bank. From the front it looked like someone had built a door into the side of a five foot high dirt bank.

The inside consisted of a wooden stanchion for milking on the left side, a pig pen large enough for three pigs on the right, and the entire back half of the barn was a chicken coop, large enough for about fifty laying hens. These hens produced almost a dozen eggs a day, giving us eggs (if you include the cost of chicken feed) for not even twice the cost of store bought eggs which, I might add, don't need to be collected from a stinky old coop, crawling around on your hands and knees because the roof is too low to stand up under, with soft chicken manure soaking up through the knees of your jeans and the stupid chickens pecking your hands when you try to reach under them for the eggs, and jumping around like their head was cut off and knocking their waterer over so you have to make another trip back to the house for a pail of water. But I'm not bitter.

Once when I was crawling around in the chicken coop I dropped my gum. I thought I found it three times.

The cow, pigs and chickens kept this small hovel so warm, even in the winter, that the smell would condense on the rafters and drip down the back of my neck and on my head as I sat milking, until no amount of deodorant would mask it. Not that I knew that deodorant existed, but if I would have used it, or bathed every week, it would have been no use. I still think that barn is the whole reason I went dateless through high school.

A typical day would start, as I have mentioned before, with my mother listing off the evils of sloth and idleness and how it was sinful to sleep in past 4:00 a.m. I would jump out of bed the instant I heard Mum coming up the stairs with the 'happy stick' (the happy stick was used if we weren't happy to do as we were told). Mum would always claim that she had called me to get up several times before, but when one has the covers over one's head it is easy to ignore – oops, I mean not hear one's call to get out of bed in the morning. Be that as it may, when I heard her pounding up the stairs I would leap out of bed, dust off the light coating of frost that had accumulated on my clothes that were laying on my bed over night and get dressed.

By the light of the winter moon or a flickering candle I would struggle out into the darkness and split seven or eight cords of firewood before breakfast. Mum always made sure we had a good breakfast of porridge or mush and on occasion would treat us to rolled oats or gruel. After breakfast I would grab the milk pail and head out to the barn.

During the coldest days of winter we let the cow stay in the barn over night. But whenever she did the barn would get too humid and full of manure, so most of the time I would have to get her in. This involved finding her first. Sometimes, if I knew I had a math test I hadn't studied for, I would walk all over the pasture without seeing her. Sadly enough though, it was rare that she would hide long enough that the bus would leave without me. I know now, looking back, that it was just her vindictive way of doing me one more dirty trick. She would trot along in front of me as we headed for the barn. She knew exactly where she was supposed to go because she had been through the routine every morning, but without fail, I would open the door for her to go in and she would turn and run to the far end of the pasture. I would then run along behind encouraging her to turn around and get back to the barn before I got the thirty-thirty and blasted her no-good-filthy-rotten-scum-suckin-flea-bitten hide full of holes. Eventually we would come to an agreement that if she went in the barn I would let go of her tail and quit beating her with the milk pail.

After I got my breath back and calmed down a little, I would fork some hay into her manger and close the stanchion to hold her. She would then move sideways as far as she could so I couldn't get between her and the pig pen. I would give her a good-natured little poke with the pitchfork to remind her that she was in my road. You would think that I had tried to hurt her the way she would fly into a rage, kicking and ramming around, trying her best to tear down the whole barn, and me, the whole time, trying my best to soothe and calm her down with the pitchfork. Finally we would both be so exhausted she would just stand there and quiver, never taking her malevolent eyes off me. I would then get the pail and straighten it out a little, pick up the milk stool and start my approach.

That's where things could get interesting, because one had to approach from the rear. She could reach, with lightning speed, all the way to the side of the pig pen with that cloven hind foot.

Come to think of it, Satan himself is quite often pictured as having cloven hind feet. It makes one wonder, doesn't it?

Anyway, the old bovine spawn of Satan would try her best to catch me with one of those lethal kicks and I would have to time it so that I could get past her on one of her down swings. Once past her and standing by her shoulder I was out of reach and could put my shoulder into her ribs and push her sideways up against the wall opposite. At this point she would realize that the battle was over for the most part and her only recourse then was to stand on my foot. It amazes me that that cow was so dumb she thought I would learn not to put my foot in that spot every day, but I showed her a thing or two about who the smart one was and would kick her in the ribs with my other foot.

With all the physical exertion involved in getting her ready to milk, I was usually sweating and breathing so hard it would take a minute to regain my composure.

The barn always seemed very humid with all the livestock in there so I would take my hat off to cool down a bit. I would then sit down on the milk stool with the bucket between my knees and lean my bare head into her flank just in front of her leg to brace myself. With my head against her I could feel her tense up just before she would kick and I had a little warning. Having my head there also let me push against her a little to propel myself backward whenever she did kick, and still maintain control of the bucket and stool.

You might not believe this, but in all the years I spent with my head stuck tight against those smelly old cows I never recall any worse side effects than the occasional gob of manure smeared in my hair. Not once did I ever have a case of lice even though the cows always suffered from lice. I made this observation to my mother once and she made some comment to the effect, "Lice have self-respect too, you know." I don't know what she meant by that, but whatever.

The actual milking didn't take too long, but it still gave her time to slap me across the face a few times with her tail. Her tail was always full of manure which she had dipped repeatedly in the manure gutter behind the stanchion. She would dip it in and then hold it up for a few minutes so it would freeze, then dip it again. In this way she could get several pounds of manure frozen into a lump at the end of her tail which she would use to try and club me to death or at least take out an eye. In a matter of a few minutes though, the bucket would be full with foam spilling over the top. It was at this point that the spawn of Satan would gently lift her foot and stick it in the bucket to soak for a few minutes. Try as I might I could rarely get her foot out without spilling some milk, and then I would have to use both hands to scoop out the big hunks of manure, hair and straw that were floating on top.

I would then turn the cow out, collect the eggs, feed the pigs and look out the barn door to see if the bus had left yet. If it was still waiting for me I would trudge back to the house and give Mum the pail of milk, wipe my hands clean on the back of my jeans and get on the bus for school.

Mum would take the milk and strain it through an old used diaper into the gallon glass jars we used for storing it in the fridge. Mum had saved all the cloth diapers she had used and would eventually use again on Quenton and Andrew, and she used them for straining the milk. I never did feel too comfortable with the idea but Mum claimed that she had washed them clean.

When I got home from school it was the same routine except I had to water and feed the cattle, haul a few hundred bales of hay home and split another seven or eight cords of wood before milking. Part of watering cattle one winter was watering Blacky. She was an Angus-wolverine cross cow that we milked for several years. One winter she spent all winter in the barn and instead of hauling water to her in pails, we thought it would be easier to lead her to the house and we would fill a pail for her to drink out of from the garden hose. This worked really well in theory. The theory being I would put a rope around her neck and lead her across the garden to the house, she would drink out of the pail and then I would lead her back to the barn. Simple, eh?

What really happened was, I would go out to the barn, open the door and call out to her using the cute little pet name I had for her ("Alright you no-good-filthy-rotten-"…etc.). She would kick me playfully on the knee. I would then go into the little song and dance routine we had worked out together. The one where we end up all sweaty and exhausted with her standing on my foot and the lariat looped around her neck.

The trip to the house was usually uneventful because she would be thirsty. She would drink her fill and then head back in the direction of the barn at a dead run with me dragging along on the ground behind because the rope had gotten tangled around my wrist. She missed the barn door by a distance of forty yards and shot off across the pasture until she got winded and slowed down. It is hard work, even for a cow, to drag a small boy over a half mile of rocks, frozen dirt clods, manure and rosebushes. Getting back to the barn was the same as in the morning, the only difference being I wasn't nearly so patient and long suffering.

Sometimes when the cow was being particularly obstinate she would not let her milk down no matter how gentle and soothing I was. I knew that if I didn't get back to the house with a full pail of milk, Mum would give me the lecture entitled "Get Back Out There and Milk Her Out Or She Will Dry Up."

One way to avoid the lecture was to always come back with a full pail. If she normally gave two gallons but wouldn't let her milk down and you could only get one gallon, it was simply a matter of topping up the bucket at the horse trough on the way back to the house. Mum wondered sometimes why the percentage of cream varied from day to day but she was satisfied with my theories of varying feed quality.

I never drank much milk.

Brown Christmas

(Sung to the tune of White Christmas)

I'm dreaming of a brown Christmas, I ask you wouldn't that be nice?
I'm so sick of sneezing and coughing and wheezing.
I'm so sick of all this snow and ice.

I'm dreaming of a brown Christmas, just once I'd like it to be warm.
But the wind is blowing and it's still snowing
The forecast says another storm.

I'm dreaming of a brown Christmas, I just can't stand the drifting snow.
I'll be cruise ship booking if it don't start chinooking
I swear I'll find somewhere warm to go.

I'm dreaming of a brown Christmas just don't let winter get you down
May your days be sunny and warm.
And may all your Christmases be brown.

The Swimming Hole

When a person mentions the swimming hole of their youth it usually conjures up images out of a Norman Rockwell painting, i.e. several laughing boys and a dog all sitting around the edge of a picturesque pool while one of the boys swings from a rope that is suspended over the water. There is a grassy bank with a shade tree where another boy leans against the tree with his eyes closed. His fishing line is tied to his big toe to wake him when the fish bites. The fish can be seen jumping in the crystal clear water of the pond.

Our swimming hole did not fit that image.

On the edge of a narrow dirt road was a slough, fifty yards across. The water, when there was water in it, came right to the edge of the road. Cattails and grass grew around the perimeter leaving open water about forty feet across. Cattails weren't the only thing living in it either – mosquito larva, water beetles, and a thousand other species of creatures and algae inhabited the water. Some would burrow into your skin and leave an itchy boil on your legs. Some would just bite once and then leave. Some would hang on, clinging to you with their little pincers until you got out of the water and whacked them with a stick. We knew that it must be good water to have so many things living in it; why, you couldn't see more than a few inches into it. Well, to be perfectly honest, it actually was only a few inches deep, but if you lay on your belly so that only your head stuck out, you could reach down into the muck at the bottom and pull yourself along and it made you look like you were swimming.

We spent many hours there, swimming back and forth across the English Channel or swimming for our lives from crocodiles, pirates, sharks and other sea creatures that infested our imaginations. When we got tired of swimming, or when we felt that some real creature had a hold of us, we would stand up and wade to the shore. If there actually was something clinging to us we would whack it with a stick and then get back to where the crocodiles were about to devour us.

If I stood up in the middle of the slough, the water came to my waist, or to be more accurate, the mud came to my mid-thigh and the water came to my waist. Several times we would wake up in the morning with a terrible itch caused by hundreds of red bumps that looked like chicken pox. They itched like mad and would have driven us nuts if Mum hadn't rubbed us down with calamine lotion.

Mum told us that it was caused from Paris sights and asked us what we had been doing. We didn't know anything and told her so, but I determined then that I had no desire to visit France if that is what Paris sights were all about.

Cattle and pigs watered at the hole and would wade out to where they thought the water would be the least toxic and take a drink. Then they would just stand there for awhile until they felt the urge to add to the volume of the water hole in either solid or liquid form, and then go back to the pasture.

Sometimes the pigs would hang around a little longer and play in the water with us for awhile. Once the pigs were gone, Marian and Shelby liked to sit on the shore and scoop up some of the jet-back mud where the pigs were rooting around. They would wipe it on their arms and hands until their arms were coated with what looked long silk gloves. Marian would hold her arms out like a glamorous lady being helped out of the carriage with her wrist limp and her pinky finger stuck up, and using the most accurate French accent she could. If it weren't for the lumps of pig manure she was sitting on, you would think she was a princess on the beach at a Paris fashion show. I guess that was what Mum was talking about when she told us about Paris sights.

As the summer went by, the water hole became drier and drier until there was only an inch or so of water left on top of the mud. It was still good for swimming, though, and is where I learned how to do the back stroke. I could lie on my back and do the back stroke all the way across without fear of sinking. It would only take a minute or so before there was no way to tell the difference between the mud and the water. Regardless of how much water was in the hole it was always a fun place to go swimming.

We never asked Mum's permission to go swimming there because she always said no. As a result, we sometimes had to sneak away from the house without our bathing suits. This didn't matter too much if it was just us boys, we didn't mind skinny dipping if there was no chance of the girls seeing us. We would go to the hole and strip down, leaving our clothes piled up on the side of the road and go for a swim. There was virtually no traffic on the road because there was nothing beyond our place except a small gravel pit.

One day, Heathen Nathan and I went swimming at the swimming hole. We ran off into the bush telling Mum that we were going bear hunting so she wouldn't worry about us and so Shelby wouldn't follow. As soon as we were out of sight of the house, we circled around toward the swimming hole, talking the whole time about the adventures we would have sailing the seven seas in the pirate ship we had brought along. To the average land lubber it looked like a galvanized wash tub, but to us sailors it was a three masted schooner complete with a jib, gang plank and a swab for the deck. We would have to wait to see if the cows were there to know if we could have a poop deck or not.

Once we arrived at the shore we stripped our clothes off, chased the cows off of the beach and launched our ship. It sank immediately to the bottom with only two of us in it. Luckily the water wasn't deep enough to come over the sides of the tub so I got out and it floated again with only Nathan in it. I told Nathan that I would push him out to the deep water and he sat down and began wailing that he didn't know how to swim. I began pushing him further and further out. As I did so, I would squat down further and further into the mud until at last I was on my belly in the mud with only my head out of the water. The deeper it appeared to Nathan that the water was, the louder he wailed. When we reached the middle of the water hole he was wailing at full volume.

With a few well phrased comments about Davy Jones' Locker and sea monsters, I had created the first wailing fleet to set sail in a ten inch deep mud hole. I had no other choice at that point but to dump out the wailer. He went right under thinking that the water was over his head and if he hadn't had his mouth open so wide he wouldn't have drank so much of it. He came back up with his arms and legs flailing wildly. His arms were still waving in the air when he realized that he was standing in knee deep water, and then he got really mad.

Just about that time, Heath, who was still standing on the shore stark naked watching the sinking of the wailing ship, shouted, "There's a truck coming!"

Nathan and I immediately squatted down in the water until only our heads were out and we felt that we were effectively hidden. Heath, on the other hand, ran for his clothes which were on the shoulder of the road. He looked down the road and could see a gravel truck coming about a quarter mile away. He made a grab for his underwear and in his hurry got both feet in one leg hole. That didn't deter him. He merely grabbed his underwear with both hands and pulled for all he was worth. He got them up just past his ankles. He turned and glanced at the truck. It was thundering down toward him only a few hundred yards away. Heath did the only thing one could do in those circumstances – he maintained his two handed control of his ankle height underwear and started hopping down the road hoping to out run the truck.

When one has both hands gripping one's ankle height underwear, it puts one in the position of having one's bum higher than one's head and makes hopping quite awkward, as I'm sure you've experienced. Even so, Heath was making pretty good time, but as fast as his hopping was, the truck passed him with his air horn blaring. Heath didn't stop after the truck went by but kept up his pace around the corner toward the house.

"Why is he crying?" Nathan asked when the dust cleared.

"The gravel hurts your bare feet when you are hopping on it, I guess," I told him.

*M*e and *M*ine *B*ruther *J*ake

Me and mine bruther Jake went a huntin. We had us too six pistols and a shoot gun between us. Are wives put us up in a sack for lunch. The road goes down us and the woods cum to us. A big rock sits on us for lunch to eat it. The wood was round us.

First thing come to us was the porcupine. I shoot him by twice with the six pistol once, with the shoot gun. I throw mine shoulder over him and carry mine shildren home to him. The road goes down us the house comes to us. There stands mine wife wide open and the door sick a bed. The door goes through me the window looks out me.

I see mine bruther's pig patch in mine punkins. Well, the door goes out me the house, runs round me I pick up piece punkin and throw at each pig he runs thru the hole in the devil like the fence was after him.

The Baptism

About a mile up the river valley from our house stood Bald Hill. It wasn't actually a hill, it was just a side of the river valley. From the bottom however, it was the closest thing to a mountain we had.

Facing due south, it rose from the river valley floor at about a forty five degree angle a quarter mile to the top. There were no trees growing on it, hence the name. Bald Hill was like a huge flat field stood on its edge, void of trees three hundred yards wide and a quarter mile from top to bottom. It was the only surface other than farm land that had no trees on it for a hundred miles.

It was a very picturesque spot which brought many people to eat their picnics in the shade of the willows at the edge of the river bank at the bottom of the hill. When the food was gone, almost everyone would climb to the summit and roll rocks down the hill.

There was never any shortage of rocks and it was exciting to watch as a rock would gain speed and go crashing into the willows at the bottom at 60 or 70 mph. On one occasion Dad took the whole family up Bald Hill with shovels and jacks, and we spent six hours of backbreaking labor digging out a huge rock at the crest of the hill. It was worth every minute. The five foot diameter boulder shook the ground as it thundered down the hill into the willows at the bottom snapping off six inch trees like match sticks.

Many young men tried to drive their 4x4 trucks up the hill but few made it more than half way.

The river came within a few hundred feet of the bottom of Bald Hill and had a smooth sandy beach perfect for swimming, clam hunting and baptizing.

So Barbara decided she wanted to be baptized in this tranquil spot where one could gaze upon the majesty of God's creations and have a good picnic.

The day of the baptism dawned bright and sunny. Barbara's friends and loved ones, and those of us who wanted in on the picnic, set off toward Bald Hill.

To get there in a vehicle you had to drive down to the gravel pit and then slowly pick your way along the river down a cow path just wide enough for a pick-up truck. It was more a trail, made by falling just enough trees to allow a truck through, than an actual road. Cows followed the vehicle tracks and kept them free of grass but between the tracks there were still small brush, logs stumps and grass.

It usually took close to twenty minutes to travel the one mile as the crow flies.

David and I decided we could take our bicycles along the cow paths that led along the top of the valley to Bald Hill, go down the hill and beat everyone to the picnic area.

We didn't realize cows could travel in such erratic directions. So when we finally wound our way back and forth through the maze of cow trails and found our way to the top of the hill the baptismal service was already started.

The hill seemed to have grown and steepened from what I had remembered. The vehicles parked at the bottom looked like 'dinky toys'

David said, "I ain't ridin' down there."

"How are you going to get your bike down?" I asked.

He didn't say a word but stood his bike up on the crest of the hill and gave it a little shove. Gravity, and the gyroscopic effect, took over and amazingly enough, the bike stayed upright all the way to the bottom. But it did make a long graceful arc to the left into the parked vehicles and committed a violent suicide right into the passenger's door of a blue car.

I looked at David. "Haven't you got a lick of brains in your head? Why would you do something like that? Honestly, some people have no sense at all. All you have to do is keep your brakes on and it'll be fine."

I rode over the crest and confidently applied the brake by rotating the pedals backwards.

I wasn't slowing down, though. In fact, I was quickly gaining speed. I looked down thinking maybe my brakes had quit. But no, my back wheel was not rotating, it was plowing a little furrow that went straight back up to the safety of the crest of the hill.

I quickly realized that the situation was not to be solved by clear thinking so I abandoned any attempt to do so.

The rocks and gravel gave way before my skidding tire, but as my speed increased, the rubber tire couldn't handle the stress and abandoned ship with a very cowardly pop. The steel rim became a very adequate runner with virtually no friction between the dirt and the rim.

It seemed as though I accelerated all the way to the bottom.

For one fleeting moment I wondered – if I survived, would I get a medal for being the first to break the sound barrier on a bicycle?

Needless to say, it disrupted the reverent decorum of the congregation to have a ten year old screaming banshee on a bicycle come tearing right through the middle of their hymn straight into the willows on the river bank.

My mother and a couple of my aunts were able to haul me back out of the willows.

Mum looked at me. "Haven't you got a lick of brains in your head? Why would you do something like that? Honestly, some people have no sense at all."

The congregation had recovered somewhat so they went on with their service.

As for me, I just stood there and bled for awhile until they were done and Mum could take me home.

It was a memorable day for Barbara.

As a matter of fact I remember her baptismal day as clearly as I remember my own.

I still picture in my mind some future archeologist finding the bicycle still imbedded in the tree, wondering how it got that high and why the paint and steel got so heat scorched.

He will look at his colleagues and say, "It looks the same as spacecraft do after experiencing the fires of re-entry."

*O*ne *M*ore *A*s *H*e *G*oes

Fell in love with a pretty young miss
Whom I swore to love and adore.
Whenever I'd ask for a kiss,
She'd give me just one and no more.
I went to kiss her good night
In the usual manner, you know.
She said with a fright, "Oh don't squeeze me so tight
And I'll give one more as you go.
I'll give you one more as you go.
I'll give you one more as you go."
She said with a fright, "Oh don't squeeze me so tight
And I'll give you one more as you go."

Her dad was a feeling old man.
He always had a feeling for me.
I know when that feeling began
When his daughter I first went to see.
I went to kiss her good night
In the usual manner, you know,
And I heard with a swear as his foot smote me there,
"I'll give you one more as you go.
I'll give you one more as you go.
I'll give you one more as you go."
And I heard with a swear as his foot smote me there,
"I'll give you one more as you go."

That dog, oh that dog, what a brute.
He was on to me quick as a flash.
He hung to my ten dollar suit
'Til I thought he would make of it, trash.
I went over the garden wall
In a manner I'll tell you not slow,
Heard a voice from behind say "Go sic him, Spike!
Just give him one more as he goes.
Just give him one more as he goes.
Just give him one more as he goes."
Heard a voice from behind say "Go sic him, Spike!
Just give him one more as he goes."

The Bus

  Back when I was five years old, kindergarten hadn't been invented and my mother had five kids so she sent me off to start grade one. The school bus was a huge machine that showed up at the end of my driveway every day several hours before human beings were supposed to be awake. I would hurry out of the door each morning, anxious to not participate in the whuppin' Mum offered me if I "didn't get a move on and get out there."
  I would make my way down to the end of the driveway and stand in the trees hoping the bus driver wouldn't see me, but he always stopped. Almost as if it were preplanned that he would stop there every day. I think there might have been some sort of conspiracy between the bus driver, the school and my mother.
  Standing there waiting for the bus and thinking about school always made me ill. I would feel perfectly fine when I left the house, but the closer I got to getting on the bus the more my stomach turned and churned until the bus came in sight. Then I would feel a lurch in my insides and my breakfast would present itself on the bottom step of the bus as the driver opened the door. He would then tell me that maybe I should stay home that day. Of course I was disappointed but I would head back to the house. As soon as the bus was out of sight though, I would feel much better. Mum would never believe me that it was a real ailment and she would accuse me of deliberately pretending to be sick until the bus was out of sight. I swear it is true though. I felt ill at the thoughts of going to school for some reason and the anxiety was just too much for my stomach to handle some days.
  Clifford was the bus driver. I thought he was a wonderful driver. He drove hanging onto the spoke of the steering wheel with his little finger hooked over the rim of the wheel. It was a very cool way to drive and I would watch his every move as he would skillfully wheel the bus back out of the ditch. I would be willing to bet that he got the bus back onto the road

on his own more than half the time. I had never seen such a good bus driver in my whole three weeks of going to school.

He started driving the bus when he was eighteen years old and drove the bus for the next five years until he finished grade ten and quit school. Warren was in high school, too, and was the biggest kid on the bus; in fact he was so big that he had to duck his head a little to walk down the aisle. Robby was the other big kid on the bus. Warren, Clifford and Robby were friends at school and seemed to have a good time on the bus together.

One day, one of them spotted a dead muskrat frozen in the ice of a dugout just beside the road.

Clifford slammed on the brakes hollering, "I saw it first!"

He jumped out of the bus, ran out onto the ice and started pulling on the rat's tail trying to get it free of the ice. A muskrat hide was worth more than a dollar so it wasn't something to give up on. Robby was there next trying to help Clifford and hoping to share in the profits of the newly forming fur business. Warren got out of the bus and walked out onto the ice and began pounding on the ice with the heel of his boot trying to break it. He was successful.

All three of them disappeared but in a moment reappeared, and to us who were still in the warm bus it looked as if they were having some difficulty deciding who was getting out of the water first. When they finally did get out, there was a debate as to who was getting back on the bus first and they settled the matter by trying to fit all three of them through the door at the same time. The debate continued all the way to school and I learned quite a bit of new vocabulary. I wondered why, after all that effort, they didn't remember to get the muskrat.

Clifford, it seemed, was quite determined to make some money selling fur and would try for the occasional rabbit or coyote too. We were coming down Fred's Hill and he spotted a coyote out in the field. The ditch wasn't too steep so he wheeled the bus out across the field. The snow was almost a foot deep and the coyote was just too quick in the turns so that Clifford couldn't catch him. We went around and around for awhile until the coyote thought he could make a straight run for the trees.

"We would have got him if these trees hadn't been here," said Clifford.

With all the kids either pushing or standing right at the back of the bus to give it traction, we got the bus out of the bush and back on the road.

Snow always presented a problem for the bus. Sometimes it would be so deep that the bus would come to a stop in the middle of the road. We all knew the drill and would get up and there would be fifteen or twenty kids all sitting three or four deep on the two very back seats.

Clifford would start counting, "One, two. One, two. One, two…"

We would start bouncing up and down and the bus would start to move again. More than once we would go several miles at a time plowing through snow drifts at three miles an hour. With the weight of all the kids at the back of the bus it put another couple thousand pounds of weight directly on the back wheels, giving us enough traction to keep going. I thought it odd, though, that it would always work if we were going home from school but nobody wanted to try it if we were stuck on the way to school. Everyone was then willing to wait for help to arrive. Waiting for several hours sometimes never seemed to dampen anyone's spirits.

Clifford had to walk once when we were stuck in the middle of the road and the fan belt broke. It was about thirty below zero and a hard wind had drifted the snow across the road. He borrowed some extra mitts and coat and set off down the road for help. We huddled together at the back of the bus until it got so cold we couldn't stand it anymore. Then some of the big kids got off the bus and made a fire in the trees just off the road. When Raymond, the owner of the buses, showed up with another bus two hours later he looked very relieved to find us sitting around a roaring fire not even worried about the math test we were missing.

Old Bus Nine it was called, and it broke down on a regular basis. One day we got to school just as the other kids were going in after the afternoon recess. That day we had gotten stuck somewhere and had to get pulled out and just when everything looked like we would get to school, some kid's prayer was answered again.

We pulled out onto the good road on top of Devil's Hill and Clifford got it into high gear. Halfway down the hill, when the old bus was shaking pretty bad and setting a new speed record, I looked out the window just in time to see the two back wheels on the right side of the bus pull out and pass us on the inside. Clifford saw them in the mirror and watched as they passed the bus. The two wheels then decided that the bus probably wasn't safe to hang around anymore and they headed through the fence and off across a farmer's field to where they hoped to be out of harm's way. I don't know how much control Clifford had on the bus but I could tell that bus didn't want what Clifford wanted. When we finally stopped, Clifford got out and sat in the grass on the side of the road for awhile and muttered to himself.

As each year went by the bus became less and less reliable. After Clifford had quit driving and my Uncle Ed had taken the job of driving it,

Raymond told Ed that the next time it broke down it was destined for the junk pile. Ed assumed that he had just been given license to drive it like a sports car. Ed drove with either the gas pedal stuck right on the floor or the brake pedal right on the floor. He even tipped it over onto its side going around the corner through a four-way stop sign too fast. He drove it like a four-wheel drive dune buggy through the mud holes and snow drifts for the next two years without a breakdown.

 I did not like having Uncle Ed drive the bus. Whenever he pretended that he caught you misbehaving, he made you kneel on the floor beside him as he drove and he would twist your ear with one hand and drive with the other. He also had the unique talent of being able to move his eyes independent of one another so he could keep one eye on the road and the other continuously looking up in the rear view mirror. It seemed as though a small boy couldn't get away with anything.

 Ed never hesitated to play a mean trick on somebody if the situation presented itself. Old Bus Nine had one single large door that swung outwards and Ed's practiced hand on the door handle sent more than one jaywalker spinning off into the ditch when the door swung open. Especially if Ed thought the offending jaywalker wasn't getting out of the way fast enough or if he thought the jaywalker was a student from the Air Base. You had to be on your toes if you were waiting for the bus, too. If you weren't paying attention he would stop close enough to you that he could slap you with the door.

 One day Ed's dream came true. There were about thirty kids from the Air Base lined up waiting for their bus in front of the school. Ed pulled up in front of the line of kids and slapped the first kid with the door, and the whole line went down like dominoes. Ed then pulled ahead about ten feet and opened the door for us to get on. He was in a good mood for the rest of the day.

 Jean was the next to drive the bus. He never spoke to anyone on the bus. He just looked straight ahead and drove with his mouth set in a grimace, his eyes blinking and watering most of the time. The only time I saw him do anything other than drive was once when a small kid threw up on the floor. Jean stopped and quietly cleaned up the mess. He had just got up to speed again when another little kid, prompted by the first, threw up a few seats away from the first. Jean stopped and quietly cleaned up the mess. The smell was terrible and we could see that Jean was having a hard time keeping his own breakfast down, but he did it. He sat back down in the driver's seat and we started out again. Moments later someone threw a tomato from the back of the bus and it hit the pole behind Jean's head, spraying tomato juice over the back of his head and onto the windshield in front of him. He thought it was kid number three who had thrown up down the back of his neck. He did not stop, but maintained his speed as he leaned over and threw up himself, all over the walkway and steps down towards the door. When we got to school he looked straight ahead and said nothing. We had to jump over or wade through his mess to get out of the bus.

Jimmy always had a bad time on the bus. It seemed as though everybody gave him a hard time just to see what he would do next. He hated Raymond the bus owner, and Raymond seemed to get upset with Jimmy. Whenever there was no one willing to take the job of driving our bus, Raymond had to do it himself. I remember Raymond driving almost as much as anyone else. As soon as we got on the bus and saw that Raymond was driving we knew that we were going to have a good time watching him and Jimmy do battle.

"Hey! Jimmy! Did you hear what Raymond just called you?" one of the big kids would ask.

Jimmy would believe anything that they told him and he would get madder and madder at Raymond, who was minding his own business up at the front of the bus.

Jimmy would jump up and yell, "Raymond, you #&@$^*&! I'm going to get you!"

"SIT DOWN, JIMMY!" Raymond would bellow.

Before Raymond could get the bus stopped Jimmy would be at the front of the bus, whipping Raymond across the face with his belt. Raymond would be so preoccupied trying to defend himself from Jimmy that he would end up in the ditch or on the wrong side of the road. As soon as the bus stopped Raymond was up and trying to hold Jimmy down and get him back to his seat. Jimmy was pretty wiry and could usually get in a bite on Raymond's arm if nothing else. Raymond would haul him kicking and screaming back to his seat and everything would calm down. Raymond would go back to the driver's seat and start the bus, trying at the same time to keep an eye on Jimmy.

"I wouldn't take that from him if I was you, Jimmy," some big kid would whisper. "You can take him, Jimmy, just sneak up on him!"

Jimmy quietly pulled his pocket knife out and then with a terrifying rebel yell, ran up the aisle and jumped onto the front passenger's seat and from there to Raymond's shoulders. With his feet dangling over Raymond's chest and Raymond's head between his knees, Jimmy grabbed the biggest handful of hair that he could and started to give Raymond a haircut with his pocket knife.

Raymond found that too interesting to give anymore of his attention to the road. So he let go of the steering wheel and commenced directing Jimmy's barbering efforts with both hands. They were both preoccupied with one another but as we hit the ditch Jimmy got off, landing against the dashboard. Raymond was able to salvage most of his hair.

They discussed the matter at full volume and with both Jimmy's and Raymond's belts flashing like the swords in a scene from a Three Musketeers movie. Jimmy came off the loser and had to be content with the partial scalp he still had in his fist.

When there were no prospects of a fight between Raymond and Jimmy, we had to resort to fighting amongst ourselves. Bruce and Earl would fight over whatever it was they had been fighting over when they got on the bus. Marilyn and Warren would fight over who had told Jimmy to pinch her. David and Brian would fight over why David had lit Brian's hair on fire. Jennifer and Jennifer would fight over one of the boys from school, and Greg and I would fight over which one of us was the better Christian.

Whenever we sat together we would discuss religion. He went to one church, I went to another. And of course we got along as good as the crusaders and the Moslems. Whenever I felt that he had blasphemed too much, I would have to punch him on the nose to uphold the honor of my faith. And whenever he felt that I had too convincing an argument, he would punch me on the nose. At that point the other kids on the bus would start laying bets as to which church was going to be the most Christian that day.

Invariably Clifford, or whoever was driving, would stop the bus and we would have to get off and do our fighting outdoors. Clifford would make us run laps around the bus. Ed made us kneel on the floor. Raymond would say nothing and just keep his eye on Jimmy. Jean never noticed that anything was happening.

One day, just as my church was about to be vindicated, Clifford broke us up and made us run laps. As I was on my tenth lap, I tripped and burned my hand on the exhaust pipe of the bus. With that, I had proof that I had suffered martyrdom just as the ancient Christians had when they were burnt in Rome. Thus proving beyond doubt that my cause was just and true and his was apostate. Greg of course declared that it was divine retribution for my obviously evil ways. So I punched him in the nose again and Clifford made us run another ten laps. We would have been there all night if Greg hadn't repented and told Clifford that we were both sorry and wouldn't fight anymore and we didn't, for weeks.

One day Arthur was being a pain and Clifford finally had all he could take and stopped the bus.
"Get off, Arthur."
Arthur didn't really want to get off so Clifford had to get up and grab him and try to throw him off manually. Arthur put up a heroic effort and it was hard to tell who was winning for quite awhile. Kids on the bus began to cheer for one or the other and it became the closest thing we'd ever seen to professional wrestling. Clifford had to work for every inch but Arthur began to get closer and closer to the door. For more than ten minutes they fought at the door, with Clifford being unable to get Arthur out and get back to the driver's seat to close the door without Arthur getting back in. Finally with an effort worthy of any gladiator, Clifford got Arthur on the outside of the bus and the door closed.

Arthur was not beaten, though. The prospects of walking home still didn't appeal to him. As Clifford drove away, Arthur jumped up onto the fender of the bus and grabbed the windshield wiper with one hand and the mirror frame with the other, determined to hang on. Clifford had no choice but to drive into the ditch and try to scrape Arthur off in the willows that were growing as thick as hair on a dog along the road.

What an awesome display of willpower and fortitude. Arthur hung on as the bus careened along in the ditch, tree branches and willows the size of a broom handle trying to rip him off his perch. Eventually he lost his grip and was swept off into the brush a half mile from home.

The next morning Arthur's mother seemed to be upset about something and offered to rearrange Clifford's facial features with a broom she was carrying. Clifford declined the offer and drove away with her broom caught in the door.

Jim figured out a remarkably easy way to clean the bus at the end of each day. He would simply stop and let everyone off to get snow for a snowball fight several times a trip. We would jump off the bus and fill our lunch kits or whatever we had and bring it back onto the bus. A tremendous snowball fight would ensue until we were out of snow and then Jim would stop and let us off for a refill. By the time we were tired of fighting there would be about two hundred pounds of snow on the bus. Jim would turn the heat up and the snow would melt. It was simply a matter, then, of opening the emergency door at the bottom of the hill on our driveway and drive up. The melt water would wash out any and all garbage, dirt, etc. that was on the floor.

The owners of the buses were so impressed with Jim's conscientiousness and work ethics, keeping his bus mopped so clean, that they praised him for it in front of the other drivers. They might have been surprised to learn that Jim didn't even own a mop.

There were others who drove the bus, too, but they didn't seem to last very long. One of the most interesting was James. James liked to impress the girls on the bus and for some reason he felt that the louder they screamed the more impressed they were. The road was loaded with steep hills and sharp corners to impress the girls with. One morning we came around a ninety degree corner fast enough to impress everyone, not just the girls. The back of the bus fish-tailed in the gravel and before he could get it under control, we were into the next corner. The bus left the road and he yelled for everyone to hang on.

As the bus went into the ditch, everyone was thrown to the right side of the bus. We hit the water in a swamp that was right there and the bus laid over on its right side. There were enough willows, though, to lift the bus partially out of the water. No one was impressed anymore but still some girls were screaming. Earl was able to kick the emergency door open and he jumped out into the water. It was waist deep on him, so he and some other bigger kids carried the younger ones out of the water to the side of the road. No one had been hurt, and as we all crawled out of the emergency door it became a great adventure, with everyone hoping for a day off school.

There was no such luck. We were only an hour late and when I told the teacher that the bus had rolled, he didn't believe me and gave me a zero on the test I had missed.

James loved to drive as fast as he could down our driveway. It had some spectacular holes and hills that made it seem like an off-road race track designed to test the skill of the off-road driver. If one was sitting in the back of the bus, the bumps were similar to those experienced while riding on a Brahma bull. It was fun. We were the last kids on the bus, and as soon as the other kids were off the bus we would rush to the back seats and James would give us a roller coaster ride down the driveway to the house.

Hayden was riding back there one day and was kneeling up on the seat facing the back of the bus. As we hit one particularly bad hole, the back of the seat hit Hayden under the jaw and drove his two bottom teeth right through his tongue. James felt pretty bad about it and wouldn't let Hayden ride back there with us anymore.

He got me once, too. I had had a very tough day at school and laid down on the back seat on my back with my feet in the aisle. I was asleep long before we got home. James could see me sleeping back there and told the others not to wake me up. He turned into the driveway and hit the first hole as hard as he could. I woke up when my face hit the ceiling. On the second trip to the ceiling, I was able to stop myself from hitting it by putting my hands up against it. I went back down but missed the seat and landed on my back on the floor. Somehow I wound up under the back seat and stayed there through the next few bumps with my head hitting the floor and then the bottom of the seat like a ping pong ball in a blender. When I finally got out from under the seat, I hit the ceiling again at least once before I could get my feet under me and scramble to the front of the bus. James and my brothers and sister thought it was the funniest thing they had ever seen.

There was one girl who was several years older than me and for some reason she hated the smell of cow manure on my boots. Every morning I milked the cow and it didn't matter what I did, the smell of cow manure stuck to my boots.

She grew up on a ranch herself but she considered herself a class above the common peasants who tilled the fields or cared for the herds and flocks. She acted the part of the princess who was trapped and waiting for a glamorous prince to carry her away. She even walked with a certain flounce and strut that just reeked of class and grace. As she got off the bus each morning she would pull a cigarette from her purse and holding it between two fingers, she would prance and sway to the front of the bus and alight in front of her friends who would be waiting on the sidewalk in front of the school.

One day when I was about grade five, she and I got in a scrap over my boots. I wound up planting one of them in the middle of her fancy new jacket. I paid dearly for it and she wouldn't stop hitting me until the bus driver broke us up. I was hurting bad and for days I tried to find some way to get even. I found it.

I went to Jim's place where he parked the bus and measured the distance from her seat, which was in front of mine, to the door. I then got a new roll of snare wire and cut it to the right length. The next day on the way to school I was as quiet as a mouse as I snuck under the seat and tied one end of the snare wire to the leg of her seat. The other end I tied through the cuff of her pant leg.

    I prayed the most evil prayer I have ever prayed and it worked. When the bus stopped in front of the school, all her friends were standing out on the sidewalk and the bus stopped directly in front of them. She got up and began her fashion-show prance up the aisle, taking out a cigarette from her purse and holding it and smiling as though she were in a Hollywood casting audition. When she reached the bottom step of the bus the wire came tight and she landed flat on her face on the sidewalk. She wasn't even able to get her hands in front of herself to break her fall. It was my greatest triumph but I've been worried ever since that maybe selling my soul was too high a price to pay.

    Some of the bus drivers lasted a day, some for several years. Some hit the ditch because of bad roads, some because of bad kids. One hit the ditch with a load of children because she didn't want to run over a rabbit that was crossing the road. Ed hit the ditch trying to hit a skunk, Robby hit the ditch trying to miss one. As a matter of fact Robby seemed to hit the ditch for quite a variety of reasons. Jim deliberately hit a skunk and it got stuck between the dual wheels and was uniformly distributed under the entire underbody of the bus. His intention of getting everybody to be quiet worked. Wendy stopped the bus, came back and broke my little finger after she asked me if I had the time, and I gave her the wrong response.

    I can honestly say that we had more bus drivers than I can remember. None of them killed anybody, but it was through no fault of their own or lack of effort on their part.

If you obey all the rules, you miss all the fun.
*   - Katharine Hepburn*

*F*amily *T*ree

I think that I shall never see confusion like my family tree.
To understand my pedigree takes more than genealogy.
Listen to my explanation, told in unsophisticate oration
As I relate each generation's corresponding correlation.

Now Adam's long posterity kept a written history
With patience and determination recorded the inaugural generations.
I will not bore you with recitation of the Bible's long enumeration
But it shows my family tree has roots, at least, of quality.

My great-great-grandpa's cousin's brother
was a duke or a knight or something or other.
He married his brother-in-law's only sister.
His wedding's the only time he kissed her.
Her brother's nephew's sister's dad kissed her, too; it made him glad
He took his family over here to see if they could pioneer.

Now grandpa's cousin's father is great-grandma's daughter's brother
I'm sure both of them are related one way or the other
'Cause my own cousin's father has an in-law who's my mother
but only cause she's married to my children's own grandfather.

Now, his name is Victor because he was named after his grandfather but everybody calls him Neil to avoid confusion, and my Aunt Susan is actually my Aunt Elaine for the same reason, as the first Victor's wife is Susan, too. Now, she has a grandson named Fredrick who is my Uncle Bruce. But he was named for his dad's father in-law so it doesn't really count 'cause he died before I was born. Bruce's mother named her daughter Phyllis after herself but we call her Kay 'cause it's easier to spell. My Uncle Donald isn't named after anybody, but to avoid needless confusion if someone names their kid Donald, we call him Jim. My Aunty Ann isn't named after anybody either but that's okay because she's not really my aunt, she just happens to be married to my great-grandfather's half-brother's son. Actually he's a three-quarter brother 'cause his mother is his father's first wife's sister, but we call him a half-brother cause he's only five feet tall. My dad is the second Victor, if you don't count Vinall who is named Victor, too; actually he is Victor also cause my dad is Victor two. My name is Travis and I was named after my dad. He was named in 1942 and I wasn't named until 1963. My brother Heath carries on the family tradition by naming his own son Heath. We call him Kayden.

With 64 first cousins, 15 uncles and 20 aunts
And countless other relates, I would name them but I can't.
Now you understand with clarity
why it is called a family tree.
Our family tree it has been said
if it has roots they're probably dead.
If you said that, you're probably right.
Our bark is loud but we're not too bright.
And when I jog I know they're funning when they say,
"Look, the sap is running."
Our tree is coniferous and it can hear.
Do you know why? It has pine ears.
I'm related to my family. It is true there's no relief
And if I could you know that I'd just pack my trunk and leaf.

Snake Hill

Out in the middle of a hay field on the Ponderosa was a small knoll, maybe ten feet high and a hundred yards from one side to the other. Many years before my time, gophers had dug into the hill creating an elaborate series of tunnels and rooms with many entrances. Over the years, somehow, the gophers had been evicted and new tenants had moved in. The new tenants were garter snakes.

In the fall, hundreds of thousands of these snakes would gather at this little hill and go down into the underground burrows to spend the winter. In the spring, as the ground warmed up, they would emerge to bask in the sun, scrape off last year's skin and get ready for the coming summer.

For a young boy, this hill was a never ending source of entertainment and adventure. For a young boy's mother, this hill provided a never ending source of other things which weren't pleasant.

Mum claimed that she wasn't really afraid of them but she managed to keep her distance. For some reason that I never understood, her reaction was totally different than you might expect. Snakes made her throw up.

Uncle Jim and I caught one and gave it to Hayden one day to see his reaction. Hayden was only about two years old so we thought that he wouldn't hurt it too much. He thought it was very interesting, and grabbed it with both hands. He had one hand holding its tail and the other holding its head. The snake was wriggling and squirming and trying its best to get away.

Two things then happened at the same time. Hayden gave a big pull with both hands and stretched the snake out full length and gave it a tremendous bite right in the middle just as Mum walked into the room. The way Mum carried on you would think the world was coming to an end. The only thing that saved Jim and I from a beating was the fact that Mum was throwing up at the same time that she was trying to save Hayden from who-knows-what, and we had several seconds to make our escape.

Snake Hill was right in the middle of our hay field. In the spring most of the snakes would leave their burrows and go off to do whatever it is that snakes do in the summer. Even though ninety percent of the snakes left, thousands remained and spent the summer basking in the sun on top of the hill. To find a snake on that hill all one needed to do was look down.

When haying season arrived we ran the mowers over the hill, cut the grass down and raked it into windrows. It was inevitable that the tractors squashed a few snakes but the mowers would just go over the top of the snakes. After the rakes had gone by, the snakes simply wriggled out of the swath and went on their merry way.

Mum did not know about Snake Hill. Mum and I were doing the haying one year and I had cut and raked the field. We went out to bale one day with Mum and I taking turns on the stooker. One would drive the tractor until the person doing the stooking was exhausted and then we would switch places. Stooking is a job that requires a person to ride behind the baler on a small sleigh or wheeled trailer designed for the job. As the one hundred pound square bales came out of the baler, the person doing the stooking would lift the bales and stack them on the back of the stooker in such a fashion that they would form a pyramid that will shed rain. Ten bales form one stook. When one stook was formed, the person would step on a little trip pedal that would set the stook down onto the ground. The trip mechanism would return to its starting place and the person would then begin building a new stook.

In the hot sun and dust from the baler, one hundred pounds bales begin to feel like two hundred pounds very quickly, and with Mum weighing about one hundred and five pounds and me at about ninety pounds, we switched places on a regular basis. A big strong man can use a bale hook and one hand to swing the bales around onto the stooker, but Mum and I had to grab both strings and manhandle the bale around into position.

It was Mum's turn on the stooker when we first went over Snake Hill. Apparently the snakes thought that the windrow of hay was a good place to hide. It wasn't. The teeth on the baler pickup grabbed the snakes as well as the hay and fed them right into the baler. The knife and plunger in the baler that cut the hay to the proper length and pounded the hay into a bale never even hesitated when faced with the challenge of baling snakes, and fed them into the bale along with the hay.

When the first bale of snakes and hay came out the back end of the baler, at least the front half of each snake was still squirming. There was almost as much snake as there was hay in that first bale. Mum had her back turned to the baler as she wrestled the last hay bale onto the stook. As she turned around and caught sight of the bale that had come out of the baler, she went straight up into the air and seemed to change direction mid-air, coming down on the ground beside the stooker. As she hit the ground she began throwing up, but in doing so she made the mistake of looking at the ground. There were snakes all over. She went straight up again and came down on the stooker without interrupting her flow of stomach contents. That put her back into proximity of the squirming bale of chopped snakes. Up she went again, flailing her arms and legs, looking very much like a monstrous, epileptic grasshopper. This time she landed on the top of the baler and coated the entire top of the baler with what little was left in her stomach.

I knew it would cost me my life to laugh at her, and even now I'm afraid that she'll read this and think that I thought it was funny. I swear, though, that it wasn't funny in the least, especially when my turn on the stooker lasted for the rest of the day in the heat, dust and with the smell of Mum's vomit cooking in the sun on the top of the baler.

The Aristocrat

*N*ature furnishes all the noblemen we need. Pedigree has no more to do with making a man better than he is than peacock's feathers in his hat have with making him actually taller. This is a hard lesson for some people to learn.

This world is full of folks who think they're better than they are 'cause their ancestors was lucky in the soap or tobacco trade, all the soap having run out some time since. They try to fool themselves and everyone else with the suds.

Soap suds is a precarious bubble. There's nothin' quite so thin on the ribs as a soap suds aristocrat. An American aristocrat is the most ridiculous thing on market. They're always ashamed of their ancestors and if they have any, or if they live long enough, they usually have cause to be ashamed of their posterity.

I know several families in America who are trying to live off their aristocracy, their money and brains having run out some time ago. They have mighty hard scratching. You can warm up cold potatoes and live off 'em, but you can't warm up cold aristocracy and get even so much as a smell.

The Hazards of Friendships

Friendships are formed for many varying reasons and one can never tell which two people will become friends, and for what reasons. Sometimes in school we will find a person who shares our interest in chess or computers or basketball or some other sport and through participation together, a bond of friendship will form between the two parties. Some of these friendships last for years but some only last as long as the mutual interest exists, and then for no apparent reason, the two people go their separate ways and never speak to each other again.

Dale and I had a friendship based on the subconscious, mutual desire to kill each other. It all started one fall when Dale came to live in Cherry Grove.

Dale and I were both out of high school and looking for work, and we both got a job working for the bishop in his construction business. We began our friendship easily enough and were soon sharing rides to work with each other. One day it would be my turn to drive and I would pick him up. The next day it would be my turn again because he didn't have a car, but I believed him when he said that as soon as he had a little money he would buy a car and would make up for all the rides I had given him.

One morning he announced that he had bought a car. I went with him to look at it.

"You are taking liberties with the language calling that thing a car," I told him. "How much did it cost?"

"Seventy five dollars," he stated with a big grin.

"You got took," I declared.

He was just as happy as if he was in his right mind. We were standing looking at a four door Datsun that appeared to be the survivor of a demolition derby. It had been painted fluorescent orange with spray cans and patches of body filler were starting to flake away revealing gaping rust holes in the doors and fenders. The hood was tied on with a yellow nylon rope which was strung through the rust holes in the fender and knotted on top with the nicest uniform bow I'd ever seen. We took it for a spin.

We pulled out onto the road and he gunned the engine, or at least he stepped on the gas pedal. Within four miles we were doing well over thirty miles an hour.

"Nobody will pass us when we're in this car," he said.

There was not a chance that anybody could pass, because a cloud of blue smoke obliterated the road behind us. After about ten miles the engine started coughing and choking and before long we were stopped. Smoke was billowing out from under the hood. He jumped out and began frantically undoing the knot in the rope that held the hood down. He grabbed the hood and flung it into the ditch and looking in, said with a sigh, "Oh, it's not smoke. It's only steam."

"What a relief," I told him. "For a minute there I thought there was something wrong with it."

"No, no," he said in his usual cheerful voice. "The guy I bought it from said that when it quits, all I have to do is fill it up with water, clean the spark plugs, pour in a gallon of oil and it will start again."

Sure enough, as soon as he had walked down the road and found a place where he thought he could scoop some water out of the ditch, it was a simple matter of pushing the car a half mile to the water hole, scooping water up with my felt cowboy hat and filling the radiator while he took out each spark plug and cleaned it on his shirt tail. We checked the oil and it was off the end of the dipstick. The fellow who had sold it was generous enough that he had left part of a case of oil in the trunk. He was right, it took exactly one gallon to fill it.

By the time we had gotten back to Cherry Grove it was starting to cough and choke again.

"Don't worry," he told me. "As soon as we begin working within three miles of home I'll be glad to do my share of the driving.

A few days later we were working at a job site near Bonnyville and I told him that I had to be home early that day because of an important previous engagement I had with someone who was considerably better looking than he was. He apparently took offense at these remarks because he promptly announced that the company truck he had been driving that day was out of gas and I would have to run into town and buy some gas and bring it back so he could get home. I did some quick mental calculations and realized that he was plotting to make me late for my date.

"How about if I just push you home with my truck?" I asked. "That way I won't be late and you can buy your own gas at Cherry Grove."

I had a big bumper on the front of my truck with a spare tire mounted on it. It was the perfect arrangement – the tire on the front of my truck was the perfect height to meet the bumper on the back of his. So away we went with me pushing him down the gravel road. I had to trust his steering because the dust was so bad back there I couldn't see a thing. I really didn't want to go too fast but I was on a tight schedule so when he started waving I went a little faster hoping he knew what he was doing.

He started waving again, this time a little more frantically. I glanced at my watch and realized he was right. If I was to get there on time I'd better pour the coal to 'er.

After we had passed a few vehicles, the thought occurred to me that maybe I had misjudged him. He wasn't such a bad driver after all. He had quit waving and had both hands on the wheel. I stayed under seventy miles an hour, what with being on gravel and all. I didn't care how much confidence he had in his own driving ability, I was getting nervous at that speed.

We got to my turn off so I stepped on the brake and turned off, knowing that he had more than enough speed to coast to the gas station in Cherry Grove. It wasn't much more than a half mile.

He was in a bad mood the next day for some reason so I left him alone. I've never been one to pry into other's affairs.

I had bought a very nice watch, one that would keep time and everything. I had never had a good watch before and now that I was into the money, so to speak, being a wage earner and all, I decided to buy myself a good watch. I wasn't looking for any old watch, but one that could be handed down to my son and from him to his son. I had shopped around and finally found the perfect watch. It was worth a week's wages and it was so nice a watch that I would have to check the time every few minutes.

At 10:46 Dale and I were nailing the strapping on an arch rib building we were working on. We were part way up the building with Dale standing just below me to my right, both of us driving in spikes as fast as we could, trying to out-do the other. I started a spike and placing my left hand on the board to hold it in place, I swung my hammer back to drive the spike in. Dale reached up with his hammer and gave my elbow a push just as I swung down, with the result that the hammer gave a direct blow to the beautiful watch on my wrist. It shattered into a hundred pieces.

I had no choice at that point but to reach down with my hammer and show him why he should have been wearing a hardhat. He lost his grip and fell down the side of the building. I wasn't too concerned because I knew there was a stack of lumber there to break his fall. Besides, I was mourning the loss of the only family heirloom I'd ever had. I gave it a proper burial by flinging it onto the top of a pile of sheep manure that was close by. It probably still reads 10:46.

I have heard that in some parts of the world, boys will go coon hunting after dark. I'm sure it can't compare to the thrill of sneaking around in a garbage dump in the middle of the night hoping to run over a skunk with a vehicle possessing perforated floor boards. You can keep your boring old coons. Give me a skunk hunt every time, the thrill lingers for days afterwards and the people you meet can tell by the glow on your face that you are a skunk hunter, one of the last of the great breed of adventurers and thrill seekers. Dale and I were skunk hunters without equal and had a reputation that preceded us by as much as a hundred feet.

Skunk hunting is a skill that requires patience, lightning reflexes, quick thinking and nerves of steel. You must have in your mind an exact layout of the dump, including the roadways in and out and any possible obstacles such as ditches, old cars, or other garbage that may pose a threat. Then it is a simple matter of cruising into the dump after dark with your headlights off, getting up a good bit of speed and turning your headlights on. The quarry, which will be foraging for food in the dump, is illuminated as well as alerted. The challenge then is to run over the skunk without running into the waste pit or into some other obstruction before the skunk gets to the safety of the bush.

One night we took my black Ford truck for a hunt. We pulled into the dump in high gear and turned on the lights. There he was, straight ahead and headed for the bush. I knew it was going to be close. We were gaining on him but there was a ditch at the end of the road and we would have to get the skunk and then get stopped before the ditch.

I misjudged how far it would take my one brake to get us stopped and the front wheels of the truck dropped over the edge of the ditch.

That wouldn't have been so bad, but when the front wheels went down into the ditch, the transmission came right down onto the ground.

That wouldn't have been so bad, but the skunk was directly under the transmission when it came down.

That wouldn't have been so bad, but I had no floorboards in the cab of the truck. (see 'Black Ford Truck')

Several things seemed to be happening all at once. The skunk was spraying and it was being directed right into the cab, all the breathable air immediately disappeared and the rags and sacks that I had jammed in the cracks of my door no longer seemed to be a good idea because they were wedged in so tight I could not get my door open. Dale appeared to be trying to get out through the front windshield, but that could have been because he didn't have his seatbelt on when we stopped.

It seemed like an eternity before we were able to get out of the truck. But we got out and eventually things calmed down and we were able to survey the situation. We were ten miles from home in the dark, in a bear infested dump. Our truck was stuck in a ditch on top of a skunk. The skunk was not dead and was still spraying and squirming around under the transmission and the floorboards showed no signs of magically reappearing. It looked like our only option was to get back in the truck and try to back it off the skunk.

This wasn't as easy as you might think. It required a series of held breaths, mad dashes, wild rocking of the vehicle and some very desperate pushing. After about five tries we got the truck out of the ditch and drove home somewhat subdued. I'm glad we didn't meet anyone on the road because I'm sure we looked a bit goofy with both our heads stuck out the windows and our tongues hanging out, flapping in the breeze like a couple of cocker spaniels. Mum wouldn't let us in the house for a couple days.

It was Dale's turn to drive one night on our skunk hunt at the local dump. His car wouldn't start so he asked me to push it to get it started. We rolled it by hand out onto the road and he jumped in. I got in my truck and rammed my big bumper into the back of his car. I wasn't very worried because he had no taillights anyway, and besides, the faster you push a car the easier it starts.

I started accelerating down the road toward the corner. The faster I went the more I was thinking that he had better get it started pretty soon or we would never make the ninety degree turn at the corner. Finally at the last moment I gave up and stopped. It was at that moment I realized that he had had it started for some time and had been trying to get away from the front of my truck but his acceleration was less than mine and he hadn't been able to gain on me until I had slammed on the brakes.

Luckily I had enough chain with me that we could reach all the way to where his car had come to a stop in the bush off the corner without getting my truck off the road.

I asked him why he didn't slow down before the corner. I was genuinely concerned about him and got nothing but a rude remark for my pains. Once his car was running, though, the hunt was on and we were off. At least he said we would be once he found enough oil to get us there and back. We rooted around in Dennis's garage for some oil, but in the dark it was difficult to see. Dale found an old milk jug that had something written on it. The first word was illegible but the last word definitely said oil.

"Oil is oil, right?" he asked me.

I told him that there were some differences but his car would burn it so fast that it shouldn't make any difference. So he poured in the whole gallon.

On the way home the car began acting very sluggish and had no power. The last half mile we drove in first gear fearing that second gear would be sure to stall it. Hitching a ride with someone after a skunk hunt was out of the question, so we babied it home. The next morning we needed to get to work but the engine wouldn't turn over.

"It must be a dead battery again," I pointed out. "We'll have to push it again."

He went on at some length telling me how to properly give someone a push, as if I didn't know how, and blaming me for his running off the road the night before. Some people can't take responsibility for their own mistakes and have to blame others I guess. To humor him I pushed him down the road with my truck and stayed in first gear the whole time.

"See? I told you that you have to go faster for it to start," I told him.

"It wouldn't start because the engine is seized," he said, pointing to the two skid marks leading from his two back tires back down the road from where we had come.

"Put it in high gear."

"It was, you %$*&#*," he said in voice that was starting to sound impatient.

"You probably ran it out of oil, you doofus," I said in the most friendly tone I could.

He untied the rope, threw the hood in the ditch and grabbed the dipstick to check the oil. He gave a pull and nothing moved.

"I think it's welded in there."

"Get real. How could it be welded? You're just not pulling hard enough, you wuss."

He grabbed the dip stick with both hands and pulled again. Nothing moved. He stuck one foot inside the engine compartment to get better leverage and pulled again. This time, however, the dipstick began to move ever so slowly. Inch by inch it was being drawn out, and as the end of the dipstick cleared the tube a string of oil remained stuck between the tube and the dipstick like a long string of syrup or molasses on a frosty day.

"We'd better look at that oil jug again."

We dug it out of the trunk and looked at the writing on the jug. In the daylight the words were easily read. Boiled Linseed Oil.

"What is boiled linseed oil?"

"I think it's wood varnish."

"Whatever it is, it's obviously time to sell this car."

So Dale sold the car for twenty dollars to a guy who said he needed one of the tires, but the next day he came back and accused Dale of cheating him.

For some reason I never did get a ride to work.

Dale moved out of Dennis's garage where he had been living and moved into our basement in the fall. He said it would be way more convenient for me because I wouldn't have to go pick him up at Dennis's place anymore. Dennis lived across from the church in Cherry Grove and was almost two hundred yards off the highway. I thanked Dale for his concern for the extra miles I was putting on for him. I'm sure his decision had nothing to do with the difference between his cooking and Mum's, or that Shelby was single and still at home. Mum thought it would be easier to keep an eye on him and his courting Shelby if he couldn't take her anywhere. He didn't have a car anymore and no one would lend him one.

Dad had a Massey 88 tractor. It had a front end loader that we used for feeding cattle and loading hay bales. One late fall afternoon Dale gave me a ride to the hay fields that we called the Ponderosa, to pick up the tractor and drive it home. Dale dropped me off at the tractor. I got on it and started for home and Dale drove my pickup home. I told him that if I wasn't home in an hour to come looking for me. The tractor usually ran pretty good but it was old and had a habit of breaking down every once in awhile. It was about ten miles from home to the Ponderosa, and when I got about half way the tractor quit. I managed to get off the road onto a field at the bottom of Fred's Hill. It was getting dark and cold but I wasn't worried because I knew that Dale was coming for me if I didn't show up at home in about another twenty minutes. So I waited. It got darker and colder and the wind started to blow harder. The tractor had no cab so I was sitting out in the cold and it was getting later and later. Finally I realized that if I wanted to get home I'd better start walking.

It was only about six miles home so I headed out, and while walking, had lots of time to think about friendships and all the things friends do for each other. As I walked I thought about how crisp and cool the air was and I realized that if Dale had come for me as I had requested, he would have had to go out into the cold again, whereas he was probably home in his nice warm bed. I thought about how glad I was that he didn't have to brave the cold again just to keep me from enjoying such a brisk walk in the dark, down six miles of gravel road.

When I got home at about midnight, sure enough, he was sound asleep in his bed in the basement so I woke him up and asked him why he hadn't come for me.

"WHAAAAAAA!" he hollered. "WHAT'S THE MATTER WITH YOU?!!"

I placed the now empty water bucket down and sat on it and asked him again why he hadn't come to get me.

"I forgot. Big deal. Did you have to pour a bucket of ice water on me?"

The next day after work we stopped to fix the tractor. I had brought some tools along with me. I unloaded them and started to see if I could figure out what was wrong with the tractor. Dale helped me by taking my lever-action .30-.30 rifle from behind the seat of my truck and leaving to chase a coyote he had seen. I tried to get the tractor fixed but I discovered that I would have to pull the top off the transmission to do it. I didn't want to do that out in the middle of someone's field. Besides, it was starting to get dark. I began gathering up my tools and loading them into the back of my pickup. I could see Dale coming back across the field towards the truck. I picked up the last of my tools and walked to the driver's side of the truck and leaned over the side of the truck just behind the cab.

The world disappeared in a blinding noise and bright light.

When I regained consciousness I was laying flat on my back beside the truck and I could hear Dale screaming at me. My face hurt all over and there was a stabbing pain in the side of my neck. I stood up just as Dale came around the back of the truck.

"Are you okay? I thought you were dead," he stammered. His face was as white as a ghost.

"What happened?" I asked.

Just as I was leaning over the side of the truck, he had stuck the loaded rifle into cab from the passenger's side and was jacking the shells out of the gun so that they would fall on the floor of the truck instead of into the grass on the ground. He miscounted how many shells were in the rifle and had pulled the trigger on the last one, thinking that the rifle was empty. The concussion had blown out the driver's window and the rear window, and the bullet had gone through the rear window and hit me in the center of my head just above the hair line, plowing a furrow about an inch and a half long in my skull.

At the time I thought he had shot me in the neck because my neck was hurting like the devil. I was bleeding from at least twenty spots in my face where glass, blown from the concussion, was imbedded in my skin. I touched my finger to my neck and felt a lump the size of a pea just to the side of my jugular vein. It was bleeding quite badly and hurt like the devil.

"I thought you were dead the way you just dropped," he said.

"You came pretty close to killing me that time. The last time I was hurt this bad I didn't survive," I said, showing him the hole in my neck. "We've got to get somewhere to patch me up."

We knocked all the loose glass out of the windows and I gave him heck for breaking the back window.

"Now look, you doofus, my new stereo speakers are going to get wet when it rains."

We decided that we'd better not go to the hospital because they would ask a lot of hard questions about gunshot wounds that I would just as soon not answer, so we went to Uncle Ed's place.

"Do you want me to drive?"

I looked at Dale. He was white, shaking and was gripping the dashboard with both hands.

"No thanks. You've done quite enough for one night."

Aunt Tanya was there and when I walked in she had a fit and asked a lot of questions that I didn't want to answer. She got the story, twenty pieces of glass and several yells out of me. The lump in my neck turned out to be a large piece of glass, which she had to dig around for with a pair of tweezers that felt like two crowbars. When it came out we all gave a sigh of relief, thinking that the bullet had missed me completely after all. She began mopping up the blood that was all over my face and trying her best to patch the holes. As she was cleaning the glass out of my hair she discovered a flap of skin and hair that was originally securely anchored to my head but was now flipped over exposing a ditch in my skull.

"OH! MY! That bullet was closer than you think!"

About nineteen years later in Valleyview I had an x-ray taken of my head for an unrelated matter, and the technician came out and asked me if I knew that I had metal in my head. Apparently there are four small pieces of lead still imbedded in the bone. My wife says that lead leaching into my blood stream all these years answers a lot of the questions that she has had about my personality.

The tractor was still not any closer to home the next day so we decided that we would have to pull it home. Dale and I got Dad's one ton grain truck and a chain and went for the tractor.

"Now remember this, Dale, the tractor has no brakes, absolutely none, so we have to go very slowly and when you want to stop, just slow down enough to let the loader arms of the tractor come up against the back of the truck before you step on the brakes. There is no bucket or forks on the loader so it is just the arms. If you let the tractor hit the back of the truck too hard it will wreck something. Got it?"

"Ya, ya, you don't have to explain. Do you think I'm retarded or something?"

I didn't tell him what I thought.

We hooked the chain from the back of the truck to the loader arms of the tractor. Dale got into the truck. Very gently he pulled me up onto the road. He then promptly forgot that he was pulling something and by the time we were over Fred's Hill we were going fifty miles per hour.

The tractor would probably been okay at that speed except for the fact that one rear tire was filled with ballast fluid and the other was not. For the first two miles things went okay but then the fluid started rotating with the tire. As the fluid got up to speed, the weight of it started to make the one side of the tractor bounce harder and harder until the tire was coming right off the ground with each rotation. I tried everything I could think of to get him to look in the mirror and see a tractor behind him, but it was no use.

I had been voicing my opinion of the situation the entire time, but my voice was getting hoarse. Even so, Jerry and Evert, who were standing in their yard, heard me and turned to look as we went by. They both saw immediately what was going on and began waving at Dale with both hands signaling him to stop. He waved back at the friendly neighbors and never even slowed down.

This particular tractor had the widest wheel base I have ever seen on a tractor and I'm sure it saved my life. Any other tractor with a narrower wheel base would have flipped over. It was all I could do to keep from being thrown off the tractor. When he finally got to the turn at the driveway, he stepped on the brakes the way he always did and the tractor slammed into the back of the truck but did very little damage.

I breathed a sigh of relief. Now he would slow down. I was wrong. When the tractor hit the truck it scared Dale and he was then afraid to slow down at all, with the result that as we went down each hill on the driveway we began going faster and faster. On the last hill down into the yard we hit about thirty miles an hour. We went across the Texas gate into the yard at that speed and then things became interesting. There were still no brakes on the tractor, there was no way out of the yard without stopping to open the gate to the feed yard, and the tractor was now airborne because of the huge bump at the Texas gate.

Dale stomped on the brakes as soon as he realized he had nowhere to go. The tractor came back to earth with the back wheels in the air and the loader arms under the back end of the truck. The truck came right up onto the front of the tractor and I pushed him through the fence out into the feed yard. The back end of the tractor came down and the truck slid down off the loader arms and rolled off across the yard, the chain came unhooked and the tractor came to a stop on top of the wood pile.

I wanted to get off the tractor and end our friendship with a chunk of firewood right then and there but my legs wouldn't work. I sat there for a long time contemplating the simple joys of life. Simple joys, like breathing.

Because I am a forgiving person, I only hit him a few times.

The second time Dale shot me we were duck hunting. It happened like this: the stress of working for the bishop, keeping the farm running, cattle fed, hay hauled, Dale dating my sister and Dale trying his best to kill me was getting me down. I knew the best way to rid myself of the stress was to go shoot something. So I invited Dale to go with me, hoping to get some hunting in and maybe kill two birds with one stone, so to speak.

My .22 rifle had been bouncing around behind the seat of my truck for some time and I wasn't sure if it would shoot straight or not so I told Dale that I had to sight in my gun. He said he had to do the same so we took a sheet of paper and drew a black dot in the center of it about the size of a silver dollar. I hung the paper on a tree with a thumb tack and we stood back about fifty yards to shoot at it. Dale shot first and hit the edge of the dot.

"Pretty good, eh?"

"That was nothing you doofus. Watch this."

I drew a careful bead on the center of the black dot and pulled the trigger. I missed the dot by four inches but my bullet drove the thumb tack into the tree and the paper fell down. I was smart enough at that point to just nod my head and say, "There. See that? That's how it's done."

Dale just stood there slack-jawed and gaping.

"Let's see that again."

"No," I told him. "I don't waste bullets showing skeptics how to shoot. I showed you once already."

I had to go back later and sight the gun in when he wasn't around.

We took off that day to do some hunting, drove around for awhile listening to the radio and telling lies, like all good hunters do, until it was dinner time. After lunch we went out to the field where there may be some rabbits, gophers, tin cans or other big game. We saw nothing. We had been listening to the radio for three hours and hadn't seen a thing.

We got out of the truck and Dale stood leaning against the side of it. I walked out into the field a few yards and he brought up the subject of shooting the thumb tack again.

"I think it was a fluke," he said in his most skeptical voice.

"Oh ya? Do you want to see me hit that rock over there, Mister Doubting Thomas?"

"No, it may ricochet over here."

"Don't be a doofus," I said. "It's just like shooting pool. If you simply hit the rock at the proper angle the bullet will go exactly where you want it to."

"Oh ya? Let's see you hit my hat then. Big shot." He took his hat off and held it at arms length off on his right side.

I drew a careful bead on the rock and shot. There was an angry whine as the bullet ricocheted off the rock and hit the side of the truck, punching a hole in the body filler about two feet to Dale's left.

"Whoops," I said. "There must have been a rough spot on that rock. Hold still and quit jumping around and yelling and I'll get it on this next shot."

We gave up and decided that we would go duck hunting instead. We drove down to a small slough I was sure would have ducks on it. We crawled through the grass to where we could see across the water. It was covered with ducks.

"Here's the plan," I said. "If you shoot them on the water you will have to wade out there and get them and then you will have to ride in the back of the truck all the way home because I won't let your muddy carcass in my truck and it is below freezing out here. So I will sneak around to the other side of the pond and jump up out of the grass. The ducks will fly away from me straight over your head. You will then shoot them as they fly over and they will fall on the ground behind you. Got it?"

"Okay. Good plan."

I started sneaking. It takes a long time to sneak through the grass for any distance and it was about two hundred yards around to the other side of the pond. No hunter sneaked any sneakier than I snuck at that time. The grass was about three feet tall right up to the water's edge and the ducks were still there. There was no way to signal Dale to tell him to get ready to shoot so I would just have to assume that he was. I leaped out of the grass with my best rebel yell. I was still in the air when Dale fired his twelve gauge shotgun.

The blast was enough to knock me backwards into the grass. I was far enough away, though, that the pellets from the shot penetrated my insulated coveralls, my clothes and my underwear but none penetrated the skin.
I lay there in the grass waiting for him to come looking for me.

"I hope this scares him good," I thought to myself. "I'm going to lay here pretending to be dead and it will teach him a lesson. He'll be so worried he'll wet himself."

"Did you see that shot!!?" he yelled. "Three duck with one shot! TRAVIS!! Where are you?"

I got up and wandered back around the pond and waited while he waded out through the icy water to retrieve his three ducks. He rode in the back of the truck all the way home and could talk of nothing else but his three-ducks-with-one-shot for the next two days.

He had tried to end our friendship several times but I had foiled his attempts and had survived in spite of all he could do. I began thinking that I should take on a safer career, like test pilot or bomb diffuser or terrorist negotiator. I can honestly say I have never had a friend who had such an impact on me or who left such a mark on me as Dale did. Since those days I haven't spoken to him very much at all. I was living down south when he got married to a southern girl and moved down south too. So I moved north and have lived among the wolves, bears and icy blizzards of Northern Alberta where I am safe.

I wrote this song to try and explain to Heath how mentally taxing driving a tractor can be. It is sung to the same chord structure and melody as "Boy Named Sue" by Johnny Cash.

The Tractor Song

Verse 1
Here I go I'm going to drive real straight to the other end of the field.
Then I'll turn around and I'll drive real straight to the other end of the field
Then I'll turn around and I'll drive real straight to the other end of the field
Then I'll turn around and I'll drive real straight to the other end of the field
Then I'll turn around and I'll drive real straight to the other end of the field
> *Chorus*
> Then I'll turn around and I'll drive real straight to the other end of the field
> Then I'll turn around and I'll drive real straight to the other end of the field
> Then I'll turn around and I'll drive real straight to the other end of the field
> Then I'll turn around and I'll drive real straight to the other end of the field
> Then I'll turn around and I'll drive real straight to the other end of the field

Verse 2
Then I'll turn around and I'll drive real straight to the other end of the field
Then I'll turn around and I'll drive real straight to the other end of the field
Then I'll turn around and I'll drive real straight to the other end of the field
Then I'll turn around and I'll drive real straight to the other end of the field
Then I'll turn around and I'll drive real straight to the other end of the field
> *Chorus*
> Then I'll turn around and I'll drive real straight to the other end of the field
> Then I'll turn around and I'll drive real straight to the other end of the field
> Then I'll turn around and I'll drive real straight to the other end of the field
> Then I'll turn around and I'll drive real straight to the other end of the field
> Then I'll turn around and I'll drive real straight to the other end of the field

Verse 3
Then I'll turn around and I'll drive real straight to the other end of the field
Then I'll turn around and I'll drive real straight to the other end of the field
Then I'll turn around and I'll drive real straight to the other end of the field
Then I'll turn around and I'll drive real straight to the other end of the field
Then I'll turn around and I'll drive real straight to the other end of the field
> *Chorus*
> Then I'll turn around and I'll drive real straight to the other end of the field
> Then I'll turn around and I'll drive real straight to the other end of the field
> Then I'll turn around and I'll drive real straight to the other end of the field
> Then I'll turn around and I'll drive real straight to the other end of the field
> Then I'll turn around and I'll drive real straight to the other end of the field

It's got 27 verses! If you would like them all please send $100 and a self-addressed, stamped envelope.

Bears

Bears have always been part of my life growing up. I don't mean to say that they were always in sight or that I dealt with them every day, but they were always on the perimeter of what we were doing. When we played outside we were told to watch out for bears, or not to go too far or a bear might come and get us.

Marian and I, before we got old enough to know better, would pretend to go bear hunting and several times we went miles into the bush looking for them armed with sticks or a piece of chrome off the side of Grandpa's car. When we got older we played games that involved the idea of bears.

One game that was played quite often was called No Bears Out Tonight. It was sort of a game of tag that involved a person who was it, called the Bear, and a home base that everyone had to tag before the bear got you. The bear had to run around yelling "No bears out tonight! Daddy shot them all last night!" This yelling gave the kids who were hiding an idea where the bear was in order to know if they had enough time to run for home.

One evening after dark we were playing No Bears Out Tonight in the yard at Grandma's house. Kay and Marian and I were running around yelling like a bunch of banshees while my dad was fixing a tire on the car in the driveway. It was Marian's turn to be the bear and so Kay and I ran off to hide in the dark.

Just down the hill from the house was a well, surrounded by a small grove of hand planted spruce trees. The trees were about eight feet high and it was the perfect place to hide. It was dark and about fifty or sixty yards from 'home base.' Neither Kay nor I were hiding down there but Marian, who knew that it was a likely place for us to be, went running down the hill towards the trees yelling "No bears are out tonight! Daddy shot them all last night!" Just as she got to the edge of the trees, a black bear stood up trying to see what all the commotion was about and Marian ran right into him. It scared the poor thing half to death and he run off huffing right through the barbed wire fence on the other side of the trees.

Marian was somewhat bothered by it too and it was some time before we could get a coherent word out of her. What bothered me most was that no one noticed that I had won the game by getting back to home base without being caught. As a matter of fact, I think all of us made it back to the house in record time.

Bears were constantly crossing paths with the local cattlemen and as a result, no one gave a second thought to shooting them on sight. The hides were kept and tanned and the carcass was butchered the same as if it were beef or pork or any other wild game. For many years, I'm sure we ate just as much bear meat as any other kind of meat. There was always a gun handy at Grandpa's house, to dispense with any bear who wandered to close to the cattle. One such rifle was known to be very accurate. I've seen my dad hit a gallon pail with it at four hundred yards.

One afternoon Marian and I were on our way back from Alvin's place and were going past the graveyard when we decided to pretend that we were coyotes. So we started crawling along on our hands and knees down the road towards the house. We crawled down into the ditch and out again having a grand time pretending that we were coyotes out hunting rabbits. We stayed on our hands and knees most of the way back to the house.

Meanwhile, Uncle Ed, who was in the house, looked out the window down the road towards the graveyard. He saw what he thought were two small bears coming down the road. It would be an easy shot, it couldn't be much more than three hundred yards. He had made that shot many times. He grabbed the gun and began frantically searching for some shells for it. He found shotgun shells and a few shells for some of the other smaller guns but none for the big one. He looked in every cupboard and ran outside looking in the cubbyhole of the truck, worried that he was going to miss his chance to get two bears. He finally looked in the gun's magazine – it was already loaded. He looked up the road to see if the bears had gone and was surprised to see that they had changed into two little kids who were now walking up the driveway. He had missed his chance to shoot us and claim it was an accident.

One day when I was about twelve or thirteen, Mum and Dad left for the day and us kids were home by ourselves. It was an uneventful day spent tormenting each other and generally having a good time. About an hour before dark I was looking down into the river valley and spotted a bunch of cows running through the bush as hard as they could go. Cows don't run like that unless there is something bothering them so I watched closely for awhile and sure enough, in a minute I spotted a bear that was ambling along behind the cows. I grabbed Dad's rifle and told Shelby that I was going down the hill to see if I could get that bear.

I had been hunting by myself many times before, though I had never shot a bear yet. Dad had given me my first rifle when I was ten years old and I had hunted ever since, so to go down with the rifle was not something that was out of the ordinary. I don't want to give the reader the idea that I was doing something foolish.

I walked down a trail that led down toward where I had last seen the cows. Just as I got to the bottom of the hill I met the cows on their way up. They seemed very anxious to get up the hill and I admit that their anxiety rubbed off on me and I went back up the hill with them.

The cows went right up into the corral that was on the other side of Mum's garden. I went and crawled into the camper that was parked in the yard. I laid down on my stomach on the bed and opened the window of the camper and poked the rifle out. From where I lay, it was a perfect shot across the garden to where the trail emerged at the top of the hill into the corral. If the bear was following the cattle he had to come up the trail and when he did I would have a perfectly clear shot at him as he crested the hill.

I waited.

And waited.

I woke up with Mum yelling and shouting and hugging me and crying like something was wrong. It seems as though I had fallen asleep.

When Mum and Dad had gotten home, all they found was a note that said I had gone down the hill to shoot a bear.

When I didn't come home after dark, Heathen Nathan and Shelby had gone to bed with dreams that I was gone forever and were sound asleep when Mum woke them up and asked where I had gone.

Mum claims that they went outside and called and shot into the air hoping to find me. When I didn't answer, they called my uncles and the neighbors to come help look for me. About ten of them showed up in the middle of the night and had a wonderful time thrashing around down in the river valley, in the bush, in the dark, looking for my remains. They claim that they shouted until they were hoarse and honked their car horns. Alvin, who claims he was there too, said that all he could think about was that he was going to run into a bear somewhere in the dark that already had a taste for human blood.

They called the RCMP to bring their dogs out but the RCMP said they wouldn't be out until morning.

Mum says that she was getting a little distraught and went to her bedroom to pray and when she was done, the thought came to her to look in the camper.

That's what they say happened. I never heard a thing.

Dad had a horse named CB which is an acronym for Coyote Bait. She was the most knot-headed, flighty, butt-ugly, pea-brained, glue factory candidate I have ever had the misfortune to ride. She was an appaloosa mare and if she is a representative sample of appaloosa horses, I can see full well why they were the horse of choice for the Apache Indians of the American Old West – the Apache wanted to be good and mad by the time they got to the battle. All of this has very little to do with this story but every time I'm reminded of that stupid horse, it irks me and I have to vent a little.

So Dad and I were out checking cattle on the ranch this one day. He was riding a mare named Lady and I was on CB. We were going east down a cut-line through heavy brush a quarter mile north of the road when a sow bear with two cubs went across the cut-line ahead of us headed south toward the road. Dad immediately turned and headed south into the brush.

"Let's get down to the road ahead of her and see if we can cut her off," he yelled.

We had lost some calves to bears and Dad had a personal vendetta against them.

"You got a rifle?" I asked.

"Oh ya!" he replied, "No problem."

The bear made it to the road first. We came out of the bush just in time to see the sow and one cub disappear into the brush on the south side of the road. The second cub came up onto the road from the north side but spotted us and the dog and then turned and went back the way he came and the dog chased him up the first tree he came to.

The under growth was so thick you could only see a few yards into the trees but we could hear the sow still headed south. Dad bailed off his horse and handed me the reins.

"Hold the horses," he said and pulled a single shot .22 rifle with a broken stock out of his scabbard.

"You're nuts," I told him. "Are you serious? Shooting bears with a .22?"

"He's up the tree, what can he do?" Dad said, pointing at the cub.

"Ya, but his mother is not," I replied.

The horses could smell the bear and were going around in circles. I was having a hard time staying on CB let alone hang onto Lady at the same time.

Dad took a shot at the cub and he sent out an ear piercing bawl. Dad's next shot killed him and he fell from the tree.

The sow had heard the bawling cub and reversed direction. We could hear her coming like a freight train through the underbrush. The horses heard her coming and started to panic. I looked around for Dad and he was already fifty yards down the road running for all he was worth.

"Come on you fool!" he was yelling over his shoulder, "I've only got one shell left."

It took no encouragement to get the horses into gear. We soon caught up to Dad and he was in the saddle when the bear came out of the bush. I was really tempted to ride right past him and leave him to deal with the bear but Mum would have whined about it for days.

The sow didn't follow us, so we just rode back to the ranch house. When we got there we rooted around the house looking for a gun that was bigger than Dad's .22. Our rifles were in the pickup truck at the other end of the ranch where we had unloaded the horses. We did find my brother's .30-.30 that had the front sight broken off, and handful of shells.

We went out and I took a shot with it, at a five gallon pail twenty yards away to make sure it would actually work.

We loaded up and rode back to where he had shot the bear. It had been a five mile round trip to the house and back on horseback so we weren't sure if the bear was still around when we got back.

We dismounted and slowly walked back to where the bear had come out. The willows were so thick a person could not walk upright through it, but there appeared to be a game trail of sorts that might be passable if a person was on hands and knees.

I handed Dad the rifle.

"No thanks," he said, "You've shot it before, you go ahead."

"Why should I go?" I asked.

"You've got less kids than me."

So with that logic bracing me up, I got down on my hands and knees and crawled into the brush to see if the bear had come back for her cub.

As I pushed the old rifle ahead of me being, careful not to push the muzzle into the dirt, I kept mentally rehearsing the motions which would be needed to get the rifle up off the ground, cocked and fired if an angry old bear appeared.

I could smell bear.

I was getting really close to where the cub would be laying. The grass was waist high on both sides; willow and dead sticks blocked both ways except ahead or back.

I could smell bear for sure now.

"This is nuts," I thought and I began to back out, my heart racing. At that moment, before I could even react, there was a rush in the grass ahead of me, the grass parted less than a foot in front of my nose and a black furry face burst through and licked me on the cheek.

Our stupid dog had followed us out to the bush and had circled around through the bush, and his sudden appearance had taken at least a year off my life.

When my heart had started, and my knees were working again we went home. I was tempted to shoot the dog just on general principal.

There had been bears harassing the cows during calving season one spring and I went out to look for them. I walked down the road away from the ranch house and began stalking quietly toward a trail that I knew bears used to get down to the lake from the bush near the calving pasture. I squatted down about fifty yards away from where the trail came out of the brush and waited.

I hadn't been there long when a small black nose emerged from the brush. He was too shy to stick his head right out into the open and was standing just in the brush scoping out the situation, too scared to cross the road. He may even have smelt me a little and was trying to see where I was. I moved a little to my right to see if I could get a shot at him when he spotted me and turned and bolted through the brush back the way he had come.

I jumped up and chased after him running for all I was worth, hoping to at least give him a good scare if I couldn't get a clear shot at him. The bush we were going through did not lend itself to high speed. I could see him clearly about fifty yards ahead of me but as both of us were weaving back and forth around and through the trees, I wasn't able to even think about getting a shot off.

He was headed right for a clearing I knew was ahead of us. I was hoping that if I could get to the clearing in time I could get a shot before he could get across. He went around a big clump of willows at the edge of the clearing and disappeared from sight. I thought to myself that the only chance of getting to the clearing in time was to jump straight through the willows instead of going around them. So I jumped for all I was worth into the willows like a full-back going through the line of scrimmage at the goal line.

Meanwhile, the bear, having got a few yards out into the clearing, realized that he was very exposed out there and decided that maybe the safest place for him was back in that clump of heavy willows he had just passed. So he turned around and jumped into the willow clump from the clearing side.

We met face to face with our noses only about six inches apart. In the tangle of heavy willows neither of us could turn around, although both of us were trying our best. He was up on his hind legs and was trying to get turned around to get back the way he had come. I kept pushing at him with the butt of my rifle and he started bawling as though he thought I was going to bite him any minute. I couldn't get my rifle turned around because it was tangled up in the limbs and branches of the willow. At about the same time we both tumbled backwards out of the tangle the way we had entered. He was able to make it back across the clearing before I was able to quit hyperventilating. I could tell that it scared him pretty good because my rifle wouldn't quit shaking for quite awhile afterwards.

I was walking home one day on the ranch and was walking down a power line right-of-way that was cut through the heavy timber. I sat down on a stump to rest for a minute and was there no more that a few seconds when a huge brown bear emerged out of the brush not more that twenty feet away.

I had no gun or anything with me and there was no climbing tree anywhere so I stayed perfectly still, hoping he would keep traveling and not see me. He stopped in the middle of the trail and laid down and tried to scratch himself for a minute. He rolled over and sat up looking straight at me but apparently he thought I was just part of the stump. He wandered over to a tree and began scratching his rump against it. I felt as though I was in the middle of a Walt Disney documentary. I just hoped that it wasn't entitled 'How Much Can Bears Eat?'

He stayed there and had an enjoyable time until I thought my backside was becoming part of the stump. He eventually wandered off without ever knowing that I could have whacked him with a long stick any time I wanted to. He sure got off lucky, eh?

I even met a bear one time carrying nothing but a small stick, but he dropped it and ran off without even threatening me. I hope I never meet one carrying a grudge.

No Longer Welcome

*I*t was a house very much like yours, on a quiet, tree lined street very much like the street you live on. It was so ironic that a home, apparently so peaceful and quiet, could house so much turmoil and conflict.

The door opened. Two men could be seen struggling together, locked in what appeared to be mortal, hand to hand combat. At first glance they appeared to be unevenly matched, for the one was old and the other young. Yet the older man kept landing ferocious blows on the young man's head and shoulders, forcing him closer and closer to the open door. The battle was waged for an instant in the doorway where the younger man wedged his elbows against the door jamb, refusing to be expelled.

"No," he cried, "please don't make me go! What's to become of me? Where will I go?"

"Get out! Get out!" the older man panted, his lungs bursting from his exertions. "I'm sick of you. Your whining, your constant begging for money. I've had enough. Get out, and never come back!"

The young man burst into uncontrollable sobs.

"Please don't throw me out."

He tried vainly to cling to the door jamb but the older man delivered a blow to the side of his head with his elbow that stunned him, long enough for the old man to push him through and get the door almost closed. The younger man, though, was able to keep his fingers locked onto the doorsill.

It's strange how the older man, who had obviously been a father and a grandfather to innocent children, could so heartlessly squeeze the door against the young man's tender fingers. But squeeze he did, until the young man cried out and extracted his fingers bruised, but unbroken.

"Your tears won't convince me!" the old man shouted. "Don't come back!"

The young man sat for a minute on the step with his shoulders bowed, stood up and dusted himself off, then limped across the lawn to the house next door. He knocked sharply on the door. An elderly woman timidly opened the door.

The young man spoke.

"Hello ma'am. I'm Bill Morgan with 'True To Life Insurance Brokers Inc.' May I have a few moments of your time?"

*A*unt *I*nez

*A*unt Inez came to live with us one year and opened up for us a new perspective on the world. She was my mother's great-aunt. We had never seen a creature like her before. She had manners, grace, poise and a sophisticated air that seemed far above anything we had ever encountered. Aunt Inez, or as we pronounced it, 'Eye-knee', had lived for years in Boston and San Francisco and other exotic places. I'd been to Lloydminster once before, so I knew all about big cities, but Aunt Inez was different, something right out of a story book.

She drank tea at 'tea time' and it was 'steeped' for a specified time in a particular china cup. She would dip her tea spoon in and stir it exactly seven rotations, tap the spoon gently three times on the rim of the cup and then lay it down on the saucer. She would then pick up the cup and saucer and with her pinky finger held out like a flag of high breeding, take the smallest sip and then make some remark about not being able to get fine tea in Canada. If the Queen herself had dropped in unexpectedly Aunt Inez wouldn't have had to change her routine in the slightest degree.

Every day she took a morning constitutional, an aspirin and a dim view of us. We were "unsophisticated boors." We found our way home from town by "instinct that was shared between, animals, barbarians and other denizens of the forest."

"Why, there isn't a street sign to be found anywhere in this God-forsaken wilderness. How you find your way about is beyond me!"

It didn't help her opinion of the populace when she met the rest of my uncles and aunts.

"An entire populace composed of riff-raff and ruffians. You make the Beverly Hillbillies look like a documentary on culture and refinement."

Needless to say, Mum had given us a list of do's and don'ts to mitigate the perceived downgrade in our social standing. I thought we were doing fine until Aunt Inez showed up and all of a sudden Mum was yelling at me for the most trivial things.

"How come there is only one pair of underwear in the wash this week!!?" and "For pity's sake, Travis, take your boots off. You are getting the sheets all dirty!"

Life became tough trying to keep up appearances for Aunt Inez. Mum was in on the deception, too, make no mistake. One time for instance, was when Aunt Inez's tea was not "up to par". Down the hill from the house was a little spring that produced the most beautiful clear water, so Dad installed a pump at the spring. We would run a hose down to the spring and pump water up the hill to a large galvanized cistern in the basement. The cistern would provide water for the pump and pressure system in the basement.

One day Aunt Inez announced that her tea was a bit off. The next day was worse, and each succeeding day her tea was worse than the day before. The pump in the basement was getting weaker too, and the day came when hardly a trickle of water came out of the tap in the kitchen sink. Mum and I went down to the basement to see if we could fix the pump.

Everything seemed to be in order until we took the suction line off of the pump. We discovered what the problem was. Someone had left the lid open on the cistern the last time it was filled; two thirsty mice had gotten in and had been sucked into the pump. The first one had gotten himself jammed against the impeller of the pump and could have been there for days without doing any harm but he decided to decompose to the point where bits of him had come off and plugged off the ports into the impeller. The second mouse had joined the first but wasn't quite so soft when we tried to get him out and he actually came out in only two pieces. The first, however, was a different matter. I had a hooked piece of haywire that I would reach in with and try to hook him and pull him out but he came out only a few hairs and body parts at a time.

When the pump was put back together it worked fine, and to prove it, Mum turned on every tap in the house and flushed the toilet several times. Aunt Inez asked why Mum was running so much water, but before I could tell her, Mum gave me such an evil look that I knew I wasn't allowed to have any fun at all that day. Aunt Inez switched tea brands that morning and it seemed to do the trick because her tea hadn't tasted so good since she came. She never bought the other brand again.

Mum was always health conscious and made sure we ate a balanced diet, including a variety of vegetables and a variety of meat. One winter we ate fish when the neighbor sold Mum a pickup truckload of whitefish. One winter we ate venison because Louis had poached more deer than he could sell and gave three or four to Mum. One winter we ate beef after the bull fell and broke his leg.

The first winter Aunt Inez spent with us we ate bear meat. Bears had been really plentiful that year and Dad had shot two or three. We had butchered them and the freezer was right full. For breakfast we had bear sausage and eggs. For dinner Mum made bear stew, but would ruin the taste by putting in a whole bunch of vegetables. For supper it would be bear roast or bear steak. A few weeks after moving in, Aunt Inez was snarfing her grub down like the rest of us when she found out it was bear meat. It was all she could do to keep from barfing right at the kitchen table.

"How disgusting!! Civilized people don't eat wild meat. I have never been able to eat wild meat. It always makes me physically ill," she said, gagging very culturedly.

I looked at her. "Aunt Inez, you have…" Mum stopped me with that evil look again so I continued, "…a very refined palate, I assume?"

"Yes," she declared. "Wild meat has a flavor that I cannot bear. How you can sit there and actually consume it is beyond me!"

Mum came to the rescue. "Aunt Inez? How would it be if I told you when we are having bear meat again and you won't have to eat it?"

"That would be satisfactory," she said. "Mind you, don't try to be surreptitious. I will know if you are trying to pawn off that horrid stuff on me again."

The next morning she was at the breakfast table dipping her bear sausage in HP sauce and asking for seconds, and every time I opened my mouth Mum gave me a look that said, "If you say one word I'll skin you alive!" so I kept my mouth shut. Aunt Inez could eat bear meat with the best of us. To keep up with appearances though, every once in awhile Mum would announce that we were having bear meat for supper and Aunt Inez would have none, but would sit and make gagging noises in the back of her throat like any truly refined and cultured person would when faced with the spectacle of barbaric savages eating their bear meat.

When summer came, Mum began suspecting Aunt Inez of wetting the bed. Whenever Mum went into her bedroom to change the bedding or to clean, she could smell urine but could not find any other evidence so was reluctant to bring up the subject. But as time went on, the smell became worse and worse until Mum knew that there was no alternative but to confront Aunt Inez and ask her if she had been peeing in the closet or something. For days Mum had been getting an ulcer worrying about how to bring it up tactfully. She finally determined that there was no other alternative but to come out with it and ask if she had a bladder problem.

After making up her mind to that effect, she squared her shoulders and marched into Aunt Inez's bedroom and discovered that it wasn't Aunt Inez at all. It was Heathen Nathan who were in the bedroom directly above Aunt Inez's. They had the window open upstairs and were peeing out the window. It was splashing down the wall of the house and landing on the window sill of Aunt Inez's room. The urine would sit there and ripen in the sun, giving off the offending odor that Mum had been worried about.

Heathen Nathan were summarily brought to justice and told to never divulge the source of the smell to Aunt Inez, who brought it up the next day and asked Mum if there was a pig farm nearby. Luckily our closest neighbor did have pigs but Mum neglected to tell her that he was a couple miles downwind of us.

Aunt Inez loved to relax in the morning sitting at the kitchen table nursing a cup of tea. After the kids had gotten on the bus and Mum's nerves were back under control, they would sit, chat and let the quiet joys of a morning in the country wash over them. It was on just such a morning that I came in from a calving problem that had taken most of the night. I was exhausted and wanted nothing more than to go down into the dark basement and go to sleep for a few hours. I laid down on the bed and had no sooner closed my eyes when Emerson's cat started yowling like a banshee.

Emerson's cat had no name but had been called many things. It had gotten into the house some how and we had not been able to get rid of it. Even when faced with an open door on one side and an angry mother with a broom on the other, it refused to leave. It had been living in the basement of the house for almost three months although we had tried many times to chase it out.

On the morning in question, the cat was in heat and obviously trying to contact its former mate in Saskatoon. The more it yowled the less relaxed I became. I reached under the bed for my .30-.30 rifle and began stalking the cat. The cat was on to my intentions at once and darted under the bookcase. I almost got a bead on her as she darted from the bookcase toward the wood box by the furnace. I waited like a patient hunter. She had to move sooner or later.

Right above my head in the kitchen, I could hear Aunt Inez tapping her teaspoon on the rim of her cup. The cat jumped up onto the wood pile by the furnace. I drew a careful bead on her and pulled the trigger.

I hadn't really counted on how deafening a .30-.30 is when fired indoors but I figured I could sleep with the ringing in my ears easier than I could with the cat howling. I took the cat upstairs, flung her out the door and went back to bed.

A few minutes later Mum came down and sat on the edge of my bed. She shook my shoulder gently to wake me. I looked up at her.

"I certainly don't mind that you blasted that confounded cat," she said, "but you should have given us a little warning. That blast rattled all the windows in the house just as Aunt Inez was having her tea. I had just barely got her breathing again when that dead cat came flying past the kitchen window. Aunt Inez is getting old and can't really stand that sort of thing so please don't do any more shooting in the house."

Aunt Inez lived with us until she died but Mum has always felt that she might have lived longer if she had found other accommodations.

I asked Grandpa, "What's the secret to long life?"

He replied, "If you don't smoke and drink, don't stay out late or chase wild women, you may not live to be a hundred, but it will seem like it."

Sugar and Cream

"Will you not marry me my pretty maid?"
"I will not wait," said he.
"You know that I love you." "I know,
"But you will soon weary of me."
But he vowed and he swore to love and adore,
And he prayed on a bended knee.
And he said with a sigh, "If I wait, I shall die."
(For he was a man, you see.)

Sugar and cream, sugar and cream.
When we get married 'twil be a sweet dream.
Sugar and cream, sugar and cream.
When we get married 'twil be a sweet dream.

But the sugar and cream, it passed like a dream.
Alas they could never agree.
She said, "Let us part. You have broken my heart.
I think it's the best you see.
When I'm gone you'll miss me a thousand times more."
"Oh no, not a whit," said he.
So away she went stomping and slamming the door.
(For she was a woman, you see.)

Needles and pins, needles and pins.
When a man marries his troubles begin.
Needles and pins, needles and pins.
When a man marries his troubles begin.

Five minutes had passed, exactly five minutes,
When she opened the door with a sigh.
"Ever since we've decided to part," said she
"I've wanted to say good-bye.
We'll never meet again," she wept.
"Alone we must live and die."
He opened his arms and in them she crept,
And that's how they said good-bye.

Let the bells ring, let the bells ring.
Man without woman is just a poor thing.
Let the bells ring, let the bells ring.
Man without woman is just a poor thing.

*H*abits

I find it funny how habits can take over your life and control you to the point that thought is no longer a necessary prerequisite for action. As a result I have always felt that habits should be avoided at all costs. A habit is a sign that one has no self discipline, that the forces of repetitive action control one's mind and rational thought no longer has a place. I learned this lesson driving a school bus.

It started long before I got the job driving bus. The spring after I turned eighteen I got job in town. Every morning on the way to work I drove down the road about five minutes ahead of the bus and every morning Leslie was standing on the side of the road with his lunch kit in one hand and his books in the other.

Leslie was one of those strange little kids who love school and can't wait to get on the bus every morning. Even in grade two he was still excited to go and the thought of missing the bus was as traumatic as the thought of Santa Claus not coming. As a result, every morning I would see him standing there and I would smile my biggest smile, say "Hi, Leslie!" and wave as I drove by. I knew that he couldn't hear me but I was sure he could read my lips and it would make his day a little brighter.

This simple ritual between me and Leslie went on each morning for a month. My job in town ended and I applied for a job with the school bus contractor. As luck would have it there was an immediate opening for a driver on the Cherry Grove route.

The very next morning I got up eager to do a good job on my first day. I started the bus and headed out to pick up all the eager and not-so-eager pupils. As we came in sight of Leslie's house, sure enough, there he was, standing on the shoulder of the road waiting for the bus. I smiled my biggest smile, shouted "Hi, Leslie!" and waved to him as friendly as ever as I drove by.

I looked in the mirror at him choking in the dust cloud and thought to myself, "This bus sure stirs up more dust than my pickup does."

So you see, habits can get one into a lot of trouble and I've tried to stay away from habits of any sort ever since. My wife Helen, on the other hand, has tried many times to get me to surrender my will to any number of habits that she would have me believe would better my life. I know better. I have saved hundreds of dollars on toothpaste, combs and other things that habits obligate one to buy.

When we got married, Helen bought me one of those oval shaped deodorant sticks. The other day I was fiddling around with it trying to figure out how it worked and discovered a little knob on the bottom. When turned, it makes the deodorant come out even more. I was pleasantly surprised to find that there actually are businesses out there that are willing to sell you a lifetime supply of something for only $1.38, but only if you don't get sucked into a habit.

Survival of the Fittest

"The full moon hung low in the eastern sky, rising once again to silently observe the struggles to survive that were played out below her.

"The glow from the last feeble efforts of the sun to fend off the night fell on the broad antlers of the giant as he stepped from the undergrowth.

"His antlers, polished from the clash of countless defences of his kingdom, shone with the reflected light. The broad flat antlers were six feet from tip to tip, the crown he rightfully wore. He feared nothing. For fifteen years he had battled any and all challengers, and had held supremacy. His countless struggles had sharpened his senses, honed his reflexes, and hardened his will until he was Lord over all he surveyed.

"Two thousand pounds he weighed. A bull moose like no other he had yet encountered.

"His regal head rose as he tested the wind. Yes. There it was, the sound of a new challenge. His huge heart began to pound as he tossed his head and snorted his distain, and readied himself for the inevitable rush. He could now see the new challenger as it appeared at the crest of the small hill. He stamped one huge forefoot in a gesture of threat, took one hesitating step to set his footing, and then CHARGED! Right up across the highway, and wiped out the entire right fender of my truck!

"That's how it happened, officer."

Lost Horse Treasure

No childhood is complete unless you've been treasure hunting. Marian and I went treasure hunting on a regular basis. There was more pirate treasure buried in our imaginations than all the treasure ever lost in the Caribbean. We didn't know what a carib bean looked like but we knew about string beans and pinto beans and figured a carib bean must be something similar; we just couldn't see the connection between beans and treasure. But that didn't stop us from looking for carib bean pirate treasure.

Bear hunting was another of our favorite pastimes. We would have been just as excited to find a bear as a carib bean treasure so we were always on the lookout for either.

One day when Marian was about five and I was four, we decided we would go bear/ treasure hunting. With Marian armed with a piece of chrome trim off of Grandpa's car, bent to look like a gun, (in case of bears) and me with a shovel (in case of carib beans), we set off into the bush behind Grandma's house with Rex, the three legged dog, trailing along behind.

If a person was to walk in a straight line east from Grandma's house it was many miles to the nearest road or house and Marian and I did not walk in a straight line. We knew that we were lost for a couple hours before Marian had a wonderful idea.

"Remember how Hansel and Gretel found their way home? They marked their trail. All we have to do is mark our trail and we'll be able to find our way home."

We marked our trail by pooping on a log that was nearby.

"Now all we have to do is find this log again and we'll be able to find our way home."

We walked several yards further into the bush and then spent the next hour looking for the log. We never did find it again and I have always mistrusted fairy tales ever since.

We looked all day and didn't find bears, treasure or our way home, and were beginning to worry we would find the first before the last. My faith in my Aunty Marian was wavering, too, and I began to wonder if being five made one as smart as she claimed.

We were about to abandon ourselves to despair when we decided that we'd better pray for help. We both kneeled down in the moss and started to pray as loud as we could. When we finished praying we stood up and looked at each other.

"Let's send the dog home," we said simultaneously.

"Go home, Rex," Marian commanded the dog.

Rex immediately turned and started down the trail. He seemed to know where he was going so we followed and before too long we came out on the ridge of a hill overlooking the cow pasture and we knew where we were. The dog had known all along where he was and had led us home.

As we were walking along a cow path through the pasture, we had our eyes open for treasure and much to our surprise we found a treasure that is seldom encountered by five year olds. It was a dead horse. One of the most fascinating sights we had ever seen. It was bloated up to the point where its legs seemed to be sticking out at right angles from its body. There were fascinating beetles crawling in and out of its eyes and nose. I began poking them with a stick.

"EEEWWWH, GROSS!!" said Marian. "Leave it alone."

"No way. This is too cool. Wanna see what's inside?"

Marian's curiosity overcame her queasy stomach and she came a little closer to see. I picked up my shovel and gave the horse a poke with it. It had been sitting in the sun long enough that the hair came off in patches as I scraped it. I gave the horse a little thump with the shovel and it sounded like a big bass drum Marian came a little closer and I gave a mighty swing and hit the horse on the stomach with the edge of the shovel.

I was totally shocked how much gas pressure was built up inside of that horse. Well to be honest, gas pressure never even entered my mind. I was just shocked at the way it exploded, sending maggots, beetles and rotten horse guts spewing out all over us. I turned to look at Marian. She was spitting out maggots and other things as hard as her diaphragm could eject them and rubbing the gunk into her hair with both hands in a vain attempt to brush it off. I was laughing so hard at her efforts to mat her hair down with maggot-loaded scum that I was having a hard time getting my own mouth cleaned out and my face cleaned off enough to see clearly. The smell was some awful and both of us puked multiple times on the run for the house.

We tried to get into the house but Mum took one look at us and began throwing up as hard as we were, but she wouldn't let us in until she had scraped us off and made us bath right out in the middle of the yard.

We had had quite the adventure and although we never found any carib beans we managed to find a memory that would last a life time. I still don't like the taste of maggots.

Whoa Mule, Whoa!

I'm the owner of a pretty little mule,
The prettiest I could find.
Got ring bone spavin on both hind legs
And both his eyes are blind.
He can kick a fly off his left ear.
He never will stand still.
I'll find a mate for that dang mule
If it costs a dollar bill.

And it's whoa mule, whoa!
Why don't you hear me holler?
Tie a knot into his tail
Or he'll go through the collar.
Why don't you put him on the track?
Why don't you let him go?
Every time I stop that mule
It's whoa mule, whoa!

I took my gal out for a ride.
The mule began to balk,
Threw her out upon the ground
And tore her Sunday frock.
The girl got mad and swore revenge
And stooped to pick a brick.
The mule let go with both hind feet
And laid my gal up sick.

And it's whoa mule, whoa!
Why don't you hear me holler?
Tie a knot into his tail
Or he'll go through the collar.
Why don't you put him on the track?
Why don't you let him go?
Every time I stop that mule
It's whoa mule, whoa!

I carried my gal home on my back
And laid her on the bed,
Put a poultice at her feet
And one upon her head.
The doctor came and felt her pulse
And said, "She's very low."
The last words my poor girl said
Was "whoa mule, whoa!"

And it's whoa mule, whoa!
Why don't you hear me holler?
Tie a knot into his tail
Or he'll go through the collar.
Why don't you put him on the track?
Why don't you let him go?
Every time I stop that mule
It's whoa mule, whoa!

*R*aising *M*y *S*iblings

Dad and Mum had left me with the responsibility of riding herd on Shelby, Heathen Nathan and Hayden. The burden of discipline always fell on my shoulders. Mum and Dad were both sorely lacking when it came to firmness and discipline, especially where my younger brothers and sister were concerned. Being weighed down with the burdens of keeping the farm afloat, the rigors of grade six and being obligated to raise my siblings, the strain was almost more than an eleven year old boy could handle. But I did my best. Many's the time, as I was raising them, that I had to dispense disciplinary action after Mum failed to do so.

Babysitting was probably the most difficult time I had because I did not have the support of either Mum or Dad, and was effectively on my own against four of the most mutinous children there ever was. Every decree was met with hostility. Every command treated with defiance and opposition. Mum was too soft on them and after she left, it would take me many hours to regain control.

"I am the Babysitter! That makes you the babies."

It didn't matter how many times I told them that, it just never sunk in and they would engage in all manner of seditious behavior. Why, I remember one occasion when no amount of threats and disciplinary action would make them do the dishes while I was busy with some reading I had to catch up on. And then to add insult to injury, Shelby was trying to subvert my authority by phoning Mum and tattling on me. I let her dial most of the numbers and then pushed the phone cradle, disconnecting the call. She tried again. I waited until she had just about finished dialing and then hung up on her again. I assumed that she would tire of the effort and give in, acknowledging my superiority and greater authority. She began to dial the number once more, holding the phone cord with the receiver dangling about a foot from her hand. I reached up to push the cradle again.

When I regained consciousness, she was standing over me still swinging the telephone in her right hand and both Heathen Nathan were screaming that she had killed me and began arguing over who would get my room.

From then on it was a struggle to maintain my rightful control over them. They were always plotting some sort of mutinous deed.

"I can't wait 'til yer 65 and we're gonna come to the old folks home and push you down the stairs in yer wheelchair," Heath declared one day.

"Ya!" says Nathan. "Just you wait. And then we're gonna break all yer toys."

Shelby was more subtle. She recruited help.

Us three boys, Heathen Nathan and I, were minding our own business one day when Mum announced that she and Dad were going to be gone for a few days and Rhonda was coming down to help Shelby.

It had been already arranged. I had no idea what Shelby needed help for. All she had to do was do as I say and everyone would be happy. But NO! She had to go behind my back and get Rhonda involved. We knew we were in trouble as soon as Mum and Dad were out of sight down the driveway.

Even Heathen Nathan, who were normally in league with Shelby had to side with me this time. With so little time to prepare a defense against the mutiny we knew things were going to be out of my control before long.

Shelby and Rhonda came out of the kitchen armed with brooms and demanded that we get to work on the dishes. I tried to reassert my authority as the one in charge but Rhonda was absolutely vicious with the broom and began beating me about the head with it. Heathen Nathan and I escaped up the stairs and blockaded it. The girls couldn't get up but we couldn't get down without getting beat with a broom. They were quite upset and were making numerous threats of violence if we didn't get back downstairs and get to work. We responded that dishes were women's work (all in jest, of course).

The two broom-packing Amazons made a frontal assault on our blockade of the stairs. I told my forces to counterattack. We threw a barrage of pillows, teddy bears, dresses and other things out of Shelby's room down at them. This only seemed to enrage them. We began to feel like the prisoners of Masada under siege by the Romans.

A negotiated peace agreement was out of the question. I was not going to be stripped of my command by a couple of broom-wielding despots whose only claim to power was superior armaments. It was a simple case of mutiny.

We thought we were lost until Heath came up with a daring plan.

He had a rope under his bed that he and Nathan had been using to sneak out of the house at night with. It was Dad's lariat. We looped one end around a bed post and threw the other end out the window. It was about twenty feet to the ground but all three of us made it down safely. We hid out down in the river valley until after dark. That wasn't the only time that retreat was the wisest course of action.

By the time I was fourteen Shelby was taller than I was and she seemed to think that it gave her license to disobey a direct order. Not only that but she would hit me without provocation, and encourage Heathen Nathan to disobey me too. Long after they were old enough to start milking the cow I was still doing it myself. I, the eldest brother, was milking the cow and doing chores when I should have been living a life of ease while the younger brothers, whose job it was to serve me, lived the life of luxury and ease and ate all the Cheese Whiz. Even Mum was on their side and took it upon herself to restrict my authority, telling me that I was not to boss them anymore. I threw up my hands in despair and told Mum and Dad not to blame me for how they turn out.

I was pleasantly surprised, as the years went on, to see that my siblings slowly began to turn into humans and became my closest friends. All my efforts were finally starting to pay off.

"When I can no longer bear to think of the victims of broken homes, I begin to think of the victims of intact ones."

— Peter deVries

When You're Feeling Important

Sometime when you're feeling important,
Sometime when your ego's in bloom,
Sometime when you take it for granted
You're the best qualified in the room,

Sometime when you think your passing
Would leave an unfillable hole,
Just try this little example
And see how it humbles your soul.

Take a bucket and fill it with water,
Stick your hand in it up to the wrist.
Take it out and the hole that's remaining
Is the amount in which you'll be missed.

You may splash all you want when you enter,
You may stir up the water galore.
When you exit, you'll see in a moment
It'll be just the same as before.

The moral of this little example
Is do just the best you can.
Be proud of yourself, but remember,
There is no indispensable man.

Emerson's Turnip Recipe

Emerson hated his nephews and made no bones about stating the fact. He was grouchy and miserable all the time and we hardly did anything to him that could have provoked the animosity. We only made remarks about his big belly when it was funny to do so, and hardly ever kicked his cat when he wasn't watching.

Emerson had worked for the government his whole life so as a result he was unemployable after he retired. He made an attempt at several businesses after he retired but was successful enough that Mum finally had pity on him and brought him home to live with us. He had his own trailer to live in that was parked across the yard from the house but he had his meals with us.

When he first moved in, it was the consensus that he earn his keep by working on the ranch doing odd jobs and helping where he could. We started out one day cutting pine posts and rails, and his job was to stack the posts as we cut them. Fresh unpeeled pine is terribly rough. The bark will take your skin off if you get rubbed by it and there are numerous little limbs that are as sharp as nails that stick out and grab you as the post goes by. Once the post is cut or damaged in any way it begins to ooze sap that dries to your skin like superglue.

Poor Emerson's arms weren't long enough to reach out past his belly, with the result that as he picked up each post and threw it on the stack, the bark and little limbs soon had his shirt ripped open and his belly covered with hundreds of scratches and abrasions. He never complained and stuck with the job, determined that he would not be the first to say quit. As the day wore on, his belly became so scratched up that blood was running down over his belt in a thin sheet and sap was matted in the hair on his chest and stomach. There were a few good humored jests made in the attempt to cheer him up but judging from his response, his belly wasn't the only thing that was getting too sensitive. It was several days before he got the last of the sap out of his chest hair and a willingness to try something different.

He tried helping brand calves but was winded and puffing like a locomotive by the time he walked out to the corral. We knew if he had to run or jump to escape an angry cow he would be done for. We had repaired his car for him enough times that we knew that having him operate equipment was out of the question. Finally Mum came up with a job he claimed proficiency in and that he enjoyed doing – he would become the ranch cook.

Somewhere in his world travels he became the owner of a copy of some unknown terrorist cell's operations manual. He thought it was a cook book.

Breakfast was along these lines – he would announce that we would have fried eggs. This sounded deceptively good. But the recipe went like this:

Take two large onions and dice them. Add two heaping tablespoons of whatever spice happens to be on the third row, second shelf. Mix in large bowl with two sliced potatoes, fifteen cloves of garlic, one cup cottage cheese and three cups vinegar or orange juice if available. Place in baking pan and bake at 500 degrees for fifteen minutes or until potatoes are half done.

The eggs were simpler. Put frying pan on high heat. Add a half cup of butter. When the butter is smoking good, crack eggs into pan and serve immediately, being careful to not allow egg whites to turn white.

Dinner was a similar recipe. Take one pound of whatever meat is available and render it unrecognizable by chopping, dicing and baking it with two large onions, fifteen cloves of garlic, three cups of spices (type and amounts not important) and your choice of potatoes, rice, oatmeal, macaroni or sawdust, or any combination thereof.

Supper was the same except more spices and vegetables. Every meal was baked in a cake pan or casserole pan and always contained at least two large onions.

"The nectar of the gods," he once explained. "Onions are the only thing man needs. The rest is just garnish."

Those of us who are survivors of his recipes can attest to the fact that they were probably banned by the Geneva Convention. Every meal was an adventure and became a dreaded event and this entire incident wouldn't have happened if he hadn't enjoyed cooking so much. No amount of complaining dampened his enthusiasm for concocting another toxic entrée. Just the thoughts of Emerson's cooking gave Dad gas and Dad had no hesitation in publicizing the fact.

After one meal Emerson asked, "So, how was it?"

Heath promptly said, "It was almost as good as going hungry."

Mum tried on numerous occasions to lay tactful hints, hoping to have him back off on the spices a bit.

"For pity's sake Emerson, the pigs won't even touch these leftovers!" or "What are you trying to do Emerson? Poison us all?"

Dad tried to cheer him up once by suggesting that he get a patent on it for inventing an "antidote to excessive longevity."

I listened to the criticisms and snide remarks about his cooking and watched him getting more and more morose. He was trying his best to contribute his fair share of the work load of the ranch but belittling and ridicule were his rewards. I honestly felt bad for him and felt I had to come up with some way of praising his efforts.

Mum had always said, "If you can't say anything nice, don't say anything at all." I felt that it was about time that we all started following that adage.

An opportunity to rectify the hurt came a few days later. It was just him and me at lunch in the ranch house and he had baked one of his recipes the same as before. It tasted no different than the others but in this particular concoction there was rice, mushrooms and turnips along with the onions. Now, cooked turnips have always just about made me gag, but these were actually palatable.

"Emerson," I said "I have to compliment you on this recipe. I have never liked turnips but these are actually quite good."

He looked at me for a second with a blank look and then his brow furrowed and he snarled, "Those aren't turnips. Those are peaches."

If you have nothing good to say about anyone, come sit by me.
- Alice Roosevelt Longworth

*O*ld *G*rimes is *D*ead

(sung to the tune of Auld Lang Syne)

Old Grimes is dead, that poor old soul.
We ne'er shall see him more.
He used to wear an old grey coat
All buttoned down before.

Old Grimes he had two lovely sons
And these two sons were brothers.
Tabunkus was the name of one,
Tobias was the other.

Old Grimes he had an old grey mare
And this old mare was blind.
Tabunkus always rode in front,
Tobias rode behind.

Old Grimes he had an old grey hen
Who laid up in the loft.
She laid two eggs on every day.
On Sunday she laid off.

Old Grimes he had an old grey cat,
He was a grizzled grey.
He chased a mouse around the house,
Broke the Sabbath day.

Old Grimes's wife made butter and cheese.
Old Grimes he drank the whey.
An east wind came up from the west
And blew old Grimes away.

Old Grimes is dead, that poor old soul
We ne'er shall see him more.
He used to wear an old grey coat
All buttoned down before.

Just Give 'er. It'll Heal

At a family reunion party a few years ago, the question was asked, "How many bones have you broke?" I suppose the idea was to see who was the most accident prone. There were several answers of three or four. One person answered six and every one 'oohed' and 'aahed'.

I was trying to do a quick count and when I said, "Thirty two", there were several gasps and some looks that seemed to question my integrity. I clarified my statement by saying, "Only eighteen were my own. But that isn't what you asked." I was awarded a Big Crunch chocolate bar and nobody wanted to be my partner in any of the other competitions.

It's not like I was ever careless. It's just that fun or interesting things seem to hurt. Bombs are interesting until Jake lights it before we're ready; then it hurts. Bucking horses are interesting until you fall off and then it hurts. Throwing flaming sticks off the top of a gravel pile in the dark is fun until one of them hits you in the head; then it hurts. Jumping off the sawdust pile and falling twenty feet into the sawdust is fun, but falling twenty-one feet onto the ground hurts. It seems as though our fun was always being ended with someone getting hurt, and the one with the fun idea got blamed for it.

When Nathan was about three years old, I was playing the part of a good big brother and running down the hill in Uncle Darnell's yard pulling him in a little red wagon. Nathan was sitting on the edge of the wagon as if he was sitting on the side of a pickup truck box. The wagon hit a small tree root that was sticking out of the grass, Nathan flipped over the far side of the wagon and landed on his head.

He immediately started crying as if he had hurt himself and I did my best to get him to be quiet. I was sure that I would get blamed for hurting him and would be in trouble. He just would not quit bawling. I carried him into the house and Mum and Dad took him into the hospital. A few hours later they came home with Nathan's leg in a cast. He had to wear the cast for quite a few weeks. Dad made him a pair of crutches out of a willow but he never did quite get the hang of them and would scoot along on his bum sliding his leg out in front of him.

About one week after he got his cast off he had his leg under the edge of the carpet and was running his toy trucks over the hump in the carpet, pretending that it was a hill. I woke up on the top bunk and I just flipped my legs over the side of the bed and jumped down. I landed right on his leg and broke it again in the same spot.

My brothers and I came up with many activities that were very fun as long as Mum didn't catch us at it.

I was always amazed at how my mother could see into the future just like a prophet: "You boys quit that or someone will get hurt!"

It was amazing! She was always right.

One of the thrilling games we had that was guaranteed to result in Mum saying "I told you so" was 'rolling the wagon.' We would take the red wagon up to the top of the hill on the driveway and each of us would then take turns riding down the hill in it steering with the wagon handle folded back over the wagon. When the wagon reached top speed we would throw the handle to one side or the other and the wagon would whip sideways and flip over. The one with the most spectacular wipe-out won. For some reason, someone always got hurt before we had determined a real winner.

Tubing on the snow on Stonehocker's Hill was also a good way to hurt yourself. If you could bail off your tube before you hit the trees at the bottom you risked getting run over by all the other idiots who were trying to be the first one to steer through the trees successfully. Darrell and I had a sure fire method of getting off our tubes before the bottom of the hill. We built a jump half-way down. Hitting the jump guaranteed that you wouldn't make it to the trees.

I thought it would be really cool to lay behind the jump and see what the tube looked like from underneath as it shot the jump over top of you. I laid down on my back behind the jump and Darrell went up the hill with his tube. He shot down the hill over the jump and cleared my face by a good two inches. Cool.

Darrell's turn to lay behind the jump. I took my tube up the hill. When I got up to the top I had to stop and do up my bootlaces. It was taking longer than Darrell thought it should.

"ARE YOU COMING?" he yelled.

"YA! YA! HANG ON A MINUTE!!" I yelled back.

I thought that maybe if I went a little higher it would be more fun, so I went up a little further.

"Are you coming? Or what!!?" he bellowed again.

It seemed as though he was getting impatient, laying on his back in the snow waiting for me to get there.

I sat on the tube and pushed the far side of the tube with my feet, giving the tube a more streamlined design. I shot down the hill straight towards the jump with my boots out in front of the tube. When I was three feet from the jump Darrell stuck his head up to see where I was. His eyes immediately became big enough to see exactly where I was. Although after that, they became obscured behind my boots and I was unable to tell if his expression changed prior to impact.

Darrell and I thought that inner tubes weren't fast enough on the snow. There had to be a faster way to get down the hill. Darrell built a bob sled out of plywood and 2x4's. It had a runner bolted onto the front of the sled that he could steer with. It was twice as fast as a tube but when the front runner broke off hitting a jump and the sled stopped dead, the bolt sticking up through the plywood had a tendency to rip one's belly open as you continued your trajectory down the hill. Darrell rebuilt the sled with one major modification; the bolt was placed with the head hidden.

I figured that a sled made out of metal would be better than wood so I built a sled out of steel electrical conduit. The steel runners were so slick and fast that from the top of Stonehocker's Hill, I could get all the way past the church, a quarter mile from the bottom of the hill. It was even able to go right over the top of a pile-up of tubes and bodies at the bottom of the hill once, while it was part of a train going down the hill. The steel runners never even hesitated when sliding on bare skin.

Having fun wasn't the only way to get hurt, though. Work seemed to have its share of hazards. The drilling rigs were some of the first places I worked that proved to be painful. When a person is young and working with a bunch of people who are no smarter than you are, it can get pretty scary pretty fast.

My crew discovered that a hard hat will pop with the sound of a huge firecracker if you run over it with a pickup truck. All you have to do is get all the hard hats out of the change shack and take them out to the highway. You then set a hat down on the pavement and send the roughneck down the road with the pickup. You then lay in the ditch on your stomach with your eyes level with the hard hat in order to watch what happens. The roughneck comes driving at about forty miles per hour and runs over the hard hat. If he hits it dead-on, there is an impressive bang as the hat is flattened. If he is off center a little bit, the hat pops out sideways and hits you in the head, leaving a terrible gash in your head that requires twenty three stitches and a real good story to tell the Worker's Compensation Board.

I felt bad about making Ron roll pipe all night with a broken arm, but if he hadn't been such a chronic whiner I might have believed him when he said it hurt. Firing him for quitting early that night might not have been kosher either.

Logging didn't prove to be any safer. Logs are very heavy. Lifting them requires a brother named Nathan to feed your cows while you are in the hospital getting your hernia sewed up. Getting hit by a falling tree is not advisable either. It takes days before you can see straight again and even longer for your arm to heal where it was pinned against the chainsaw.

Quenton proved to be very hazardous too. He and I were limbing a tree with chainsaws. I was walking down one side of the tree with my chainsaw, cutting the limbs off that were on my side of the tree. Quenton was on the other side of the tree with his saw. As he was cutting, the chain on his saw broke and came right off of his saw. He turned and pretended to trip and stuck the bar of his chainless saw right up between my legs and pulled the throttle. All I knew was that there was a roaring chainsaw between my legs and I fell to the ground screaming and bleeding all over the place before I realized that I wasn't hurt at all. I still owe him for that one.

I had an opportunity to get even a few days later when he fell a tree and it flipped back and dropped on him, pinning him to the ground. It would have killed him if there hadn't been a deadfall tree under the snow that took the brunt of the impact. I saw him there pinned under the tree but I panicked and got him out.

The day I lost my finger, Quenton and I were trying to start a planer mill. There was a serious snow storm on and the belts kept coming off because of the snow on the pulleys and the engine would keep stalling. When we finally got the thing so it would keep running, I realized I had forgotten to take a cap off the sawdust blower. All I had to do was reach in under a spinning knife and pull it off. There was no reason to shut the mill down after we had just got it running.

I reached in and grabbed the cap. The suction on the back side of the cap forced me to lift against it quite hard. When the cap came off, the suction disappeared but I was still lifting and my hand went up into the knife. I pulled my hand out and I could feel that there were multiple pieces in my glove. I didn't want to take the glove off and lose the pieces. Quenton came around the mill and fainted. At least, I didn't see him again until after I went to the office and stopped the bleeding and got the boss to phone the hospital. Quenton showed up at that point and drove me into town. It took over an hour to get to the hospital.

When we got there I went in and asked where the doctor was. I was told by the nurse that she wanted to look at it first to see if it was serious enough to bother the doctor.

"Didn't we phone you and tell you there were amputations?"

"Yes but sometimes people exaggerate."

She did think it was serious enough and called the doctor. He obviously thought it wasn't too serious because he took longer to get there than it took us. He took one look at it and said, "I'm not touching it. You go to Grande Prairie."

We got back in the truck and pulled back out onto the road. Dad happened to be driving by. We flagged him down and he drove me to Grande Prairie.

I walked into the emergency room and the nurse asked me what the matter was.

"Minor lacerations. I think I have all the pieces," I said, unwrapping it and showing her.

My hand was getting uncomfortable by the time a doctor looked at it, almost five hours from the time I first hurt it.

Losing a digit is not something I would recommend but I did gain a better appreciation of what George felt like when I cut his toes off.

Byron had asked me to do some cultivating for him when I was about fifteen. George came out to the field to help me hook the tractor to the cultivator. It would have been an easy thing to accomplish except for two problems. We had to back downhill to the cultivator, and the tractor had no brakes what-so-ever.

We tried several times to back up to the cultivator, but each time, the tractor would roll too far and smash into the cultivator. We decided to place a rock behind the rear wheel that would stop the tractor at the right point. It worked, but now we discovered that the hitch of the tractor was lower than the cultivator. George figured that if he stood on the cultivator hitch he could hold it at the right level. I pulled the tractor ahead a little and he stood on the hitch of the cultivator. George's weight brought it down to the right level. I started to back up again but this time the rock didn't stop the tractor. Instead, the tractor rolled up over the rock and the hitch of the tractor went up and then came down on top of George's foot and the tractor didn't stop until the hitch was stopped by the cultivator hitch. Luckily, George's foot was still stuck between the two hitches and it cushioned the impact so that neither machine was damaged.

On the way to the hospital, he kept saying that his toes were gone and was getting pretty loud about it, almost as if he thought I was hard of hearing. I could hear him very clearly all the way to town. All I could think about was having to go back and look through the dirt to find his toes. I didn't have to, though, because he found them himself, rolling around in the end of his sock.

There were several bones in his foot and ankle that weren't in peak condition either. But he recovered and went on to eventually be my driller on the rigs for awhile, and was able to get revenge on me to some extent even though it was mostly his fault for offering to help.

It is said that a wise person learns from his mistakes and a wiser one will learn from the mistakes of others. If we are wise we can learn something new every day. I made this observation to my Dad as he was taking me to the hospital one day. He looked at me and remarked, "That may be true for most people, but in your case, you just get a little less stupid every day."

I don't mind being educated in the school of hard knocks. It's all these refresher courses that I keep taking that bother me. So, in the hopes of helping in your education, keep in mind the following pieces of advice that I have learned from experience.

1. When skiing behind the truck and Tom is driving, don't tie the rope around your waist. And when you wipe out, don't holler 'Whoa.' He will think you hollered 'go' and will speed up and drag you all the way down the road as you bounce from one ditch to the other.

2. Don't stand directly behind the bull when using a short-handled stock prod.

3. Make sure there is someone who can drag you out of the chute when the bull starts backing back down the chute after you have used the short-handled stock prod and are busy clutching the area affected by the bull's kick.

4. When hanging onto someone's bumper and skiing behind them down a snow covered road, let go before you get to the dry pavement.

5. Don't ride your bike straight down the side of the river valley into the river. (see 'The Baptism')

6. Before carrying a pump liner and dropping it on your foot, change your cowboy boots for ones with steel toes. If you don't, then when you are taking your boot off and pouring the blood out, Alvin, who is waiting in the dog house will say, "That's the bad thing about being the driller. You can't show the pain or you risk becoming a mere mortal in the eyes of your crew."

7. Don't show the roughneck how tough you are by lifting the end of a 6¼ inch drill collar. This will produce a series of noises and pains in the lower back that last for many years and evoke disparaging comments from every doctor who x-rays you for the next twenty years.

8. When riding a motorcycle for the first time, stay away from barbed wire fences, or at least gear down a little.

9. Don't try to jump over a barbed wire fence if it is electrified and your pants are too baggy and the ground is muddy.

10. If it took both your dad and you to close a chain boomer with a six-foot snipe, don't pull the snipe towards your ribs when you try to undo it.

11. When sitting on the foot of the hospital bed while recovering from the latest injury, don't prop your feet up on a rolling trolley. As the trolley rolls away from you and your feet come off the trolley, the bandages around your stomach will prevent you from regaining your balance and you will smash your teeth out on the edge of the trolley and you will be very embarrassed trying to explain to the nurse why there is blood on the floor all the way down the hallway to the washroom.

12. If you are checking cows in the dark with a flashlight and the dog runs cowering behind you, there will be a mad cow coming out of the darkness after the dog. Leave the dog.

13. If you are carrying a cow's calf back to the barn, you cannot outrun the angry cow in the snow. Drop the calf.

14. When wrestling a long-horned steer at college, keep your face away from the horns. A broken cheek bone makes it difficult to concentrate on the exam the next day.

15. When playing catcher at a ball game, wear a mask when Louis is batting. He throws the bat. I would also recommend that you play with a real bat and not a piece of angle iron like we were.

16. Don't tease Marian when she is carrying a weapon of any sort. This includes milk pails.

17. When you are chopping a hole in the river ice so the cows can drink, and when the cows walk out on the ice and break through, once you are out of the water, don't pour the water out of your rubber boots if it is twenty below zero and it is a mile back to the house. The water will act as an insulator and the frost bite won't be nearly as bad.

18. Gravel isn't as soft as it looks. Don't jump off the top of the stock pile thinking that the little gravel pile at the bottom is as soft as it looks.

19. Catching flaming logs in the dark that other Boy Scouts are pulling out of the fire and throwing at you, is not as easy as you might think.

20. Shooting a high powered rifle inside the house is hard on the ears.

21. After your dad has shot a big brown bear, don't assume it is dead just because it is laying still. Whatever you do, don't turn your back on it; it will get up and try to bite you and claw you one more time.

22. 'Just give 'er, it'll heal' is not a good motto.

These are a few of the things I have learned about life's hazards. I hope they help you out. They are certainly things I wish I'd known ahead of time.

Never go out to meet trouble. If you will just sit still, nine cases out of ten someone will intercept it before it reaches you.
- Calvin Coolidge

*H*atch's *R*endition of "*L*ast *K*iss...mas"

(sung to the tune of Last Kiss)

We were out on a date in my daddy's car,
We hadn't driven very far.
There in the road, straight ahead,
A sleigh was stalled. Rudolph was dead.
I couldn't stop so I swerved to the right,
I'll never forget the deer that night.
The crying tires, the bustin' glass,
The road kill deer that I saw last.

Oh where, oh where can my stocking be.
Santa Claus is mad at me.
We butchered Rudolph but what could we do?
Got Christmas dinner cooking on the bar-be-que

When I woke up the snow was coming down.
There was Santa lyin' on the ground.
I raised his head, he was breathing clear.
I left him there and went to load the deer.
My grill was bent, it was full of hair,
There were reindeer layin' everywhere.
There were six reindeer loaded in my truck.
Prancer would make a trophy buck.
Old Nick came to and as I drove away.
He was writing down the number on my licence plate.

Oh where, oh where can my stocking be.
Santa Claus is mad at me.
We butchered Rudolph but what could we do?
Got Christmas dinner cooking on the bar-be-que.

No Talent

(sung to the same tune as A Boy Named Sue)

By the time you listen to this song,
you'll realize that something's wrong,
And discover this song has no melody.
But don't feel bad cause that's okay.
See, it was really meant that way.
It's a song written especially for me.

It really is no fault of mine, I've practiced hard and I've been tryin'.
As a matter of fact I've tried everything.
I guess this is how it's got to be, a song without a melody,
With the talent I have, it's the only one I can sing.

Yes I have tried year after year,
to start my musical career,
They say all you have to do is just believe.
Many people have heard me try,
and it hurts so bad it makes me cry,
When I see them cringe, then all get up and leave.

I've practiced hard so I'd go far, to be a country music star.
I tried everything to get ahead.
But I have no talent as you can see,
so I guess there's just one course for me.
I guess I'll have to be a rock star instead

Back ground music changes to fifties rock beat with same chord pattern

Just take a look at old Bob Dillan, I tell you man, he's made a killin'
And it certainly ain't his voice that people like.
And old Mick Jagger from the Rolling Stones,
with pneumatic lips and geriatric bones
Why, he don't need a cane when he's got the mike.

Then there's these other new rock bands,
they play some noise that I can't stand,
I tell you some of that stuff is pretty rough.
They don't worry about melody,
and if they happen to sing off key
They think that they're not yellin' loud enough

Then there's this music that they call rap,
Is it any coincidence, it rhymes with crap?
I think they get their rhymes from mother goose
Some of that stuff is pretty bad.
When you think about it, it's kind of sad,
'Cause none of them are as good as Dr. Seuss.

And the way these women are dressed to kill,
why they don't have to show no skill
If they got something else that they can show.
So maybe there's still is hope for me,
in the rock music industry.
If you have no talent there's still one place to go
With a little luck and a little cash,
Lots of volume and lots of flash.
If you have no talent you can still put on a show.
With a little luck and a little cash,
Lots of volume and lots of flash.
If you have no talent you can still put on a show.

*W*ipe *O*ut

*M*y Aunty Beeno was about one year older than me. I called her Beeno because it really irritated her. She would also get very embarrassed in front of her friends at school if I called her Aunty Beeno. So every chance I had, I did. She'd beat me later for it but it was worth it.

She felt it was her duty to beat me up every day or so because I was quite a bit smarter than her and she felt intimidated. If she read this she would almost certainly argue the point but you'll have to trust me on it for a minute, as I will soon give evidence supporting my view point.

We had a bicycle that occasionally had wheels on it. One summer day when we were about nine and ten years old, I stole a wheel that had air in it off Jim's bike and put it on the front of the bike, replacing the one of ours that didn't have air. I did not tighten the nuts because I knew we would have to get the wheel back on Jim's bike before he got home and it would take effort to find a wrench, take the wrench back, etc., etc.

My Uncle Alvin lived down at the bottom of the hill a mile away and was on holidays, so Beeno and I decided to take the bike down to Alvin's and get some of the candy he had left for us.

We knew he had left it especially for us, because it was hidden in a duffel bag under a pile of boxes at the back of his porch.

Anyway, we started out down the hill on the bike with Beeno doing all the pedaling (intelligence exhibit A) and me riding behind on the long banana seat.

Now, the gravel road down the hill past the graveyard had occasional rocks that the grader bounced over, leaving speed bump shaped piles of gravel where the rock lifted the grader blade. The hill was steep, long and straight, so a kid on a bike could get lots of speed.

Halfway down the hill I could tell by the gravel going by below my feet that we were going at least a hundred miles per hour, and a hundred miles per hour is pretty fast for a nine year old kid, especially for one hanging on behind his incompetent ten year old aunt.

Beeno yelled "Hang on, we're gonna jump the rock bump!" (intelligence exhibit B)

At that moment I remembered the loose wheel nuts and screamed my objections as loudly as I could in her left ear. But it was too late. The bike was already airborne. Out of the corner of my eye I caught sight of our front wheel making a break for the safety of the trees, and then the bike landed and stopped. Beeno and I were once more airborne.

I distinctly recall thinking, "This is her fault. I will not pay for her mistakes."

So I grabbed the back of her shirt with both hands. When we touched down again, I had both of my knees in the small of her back with my feet up out of the gravel and both my hands clutching the fabric of her shirt behind her shoulder blades.

She didn't slide in the gravel quite as smoothly as a sled would have, but I was able to stay up out of the gravel until we slid to a stop without getting hurt at all. When we finally stopped, I dismounted and started for home as fast as my legs could carry me. I knew that if she could still walk, I was a dead man.

If you can keep your head while those around you are losing theirs, perhaps you do not understand the situation.
— Nelson Boswell

UFA Meeting

The room was crowded with people chatting and trying to find a place to sit in the rows of stacking chairs that had been set out. The chairman stood and walked over to stand behind the podium. The noise slowly ebbed and died. The chairman tapped the microphone with his finger to see if it was turned on. It wasn't, so he leaned forward and spoke directly into it.

"Gentlemen, please take your seats and we'll call this meeting of U.F.A. to order. If there is anyone in the back who can't hear me, please raise your hand."

Three men in the back row waved at him.

"Good. Our first item of business is to introduce our newest member, Dave. Dave, can you come forward and tell us about yourself? Don't be shy. We are all here for the same reason, and we've all had to bare ourselves to be able to deal with it."

Dave walked to the front of the room. He was in his early forties with slightly graying hair partially hid beneath a ball cap bearing the label "Nothing runs like a Deere." His flannel shirt was frayed at the collar and one of his cuff buttons was missing. He stood at the front of the room staring at a spot on the floor about four feet in front of him. There was an awkward silence for a few moments before he began to speak.

"My…," he paused. "My name is Dave."

He took his hat off and began to twist it into a ball in front of him. He still couldn't bring himself to look at his audience. There was a long silence as he gathered his nerve to voice the confession he knew his audience was expecting.

"My name is Dave," he began again, "and I'm… a … a… a farmer."

A murmur of sympathetic "ahh's" went through the crowd.

Dave forged ahead with his story, relief flooding through him as he unloaded his mental burden.

"I've been farming for eighteen years and I can't quit. I don't want to blame anyone but myself, but my father was a farmer, too, and gave me rides on his Cockshutt when I was only three years old."

There was a sharp intake of breath from the crowd.

Dave looked up quickly and said, "No, no, don't get me wrong. I'm not blaming him. I don't hold it against him. They didn't know any better back then. Almost everyone I knew as a youngster, farmed. When I was young I didn't realize the consequences. I learned how to milk a cow and there was times I would skip school in the fall to drive combine."

Dave looked up again. A few solemn-faced men met his gaze and nodded. They understood what he was going through. That thought gave him the courage to go on.

"I thought I could beat it once. When I got out of high school I went to college and became an electrician. I married a good woman and I was able to hide my past from her. I got a good job and was making good money but I started slowing down as I drove past the New Holland dealer. Then one day I stopped. I knew I shouldn't go in but I told myself it won't hurt to just look. One thing led to another and before I realized how serious it was, I had a subscription to the Western Producer. It just got worse. I even had the latest copy of the Cattleman's magazine hid under my mattress."

"I thought I could handle it, I wasn't hooked. I thought I was immune to the hard stuff but when a half section came up for sale just a half hour out of town I just couldn't help it! There were no rocks on it!"

Dave broke down in tears, the sobs coming uncontrollably. The chairman stepped forward and put his arm around the back of Dave's shoulders. He said nothing, but Dave knew and could feel the empathy. The chairman wasn't the only man in the room whose eyes were moist. Only the hardest of hearts were unaffected by Dave's tragic tale.

Dave finally regained his composure, and continued. "Before long I was in debt. It was so easy. Just used equipment, I told myself, I won't go beyond that. But one dark night there was a knock on my door. It was my neighbour. He wanted me to rent three quarters from him. I told him no, I just wouldn't do it but he argued with me and in the end he broke my will and I rented the land and bought a new John Deere."

Once again the crowd could not contain its gasp of horror.

"I couldn't hide it any longer from my wife," he struggled on, "but she loved me and took it very well. She even went to work at Peavey Mart to try and help me but it was no use. I was missing days at work and coming in late. My boss confronted me with it one day. At first he thought I was just an alcoholic or a junky but when the truth came out that I was farming he had to let me go."

"I worked at any job I could find to support my farming. I even…," he faltered, "I even drove truck."

"Gasp!" Several muttered whispers went around the hall as they realized just how low Dave had sunk.

"My wife could no longer stay. She took the kids and said, 'It's the farm or me.'"

He sobbed once, his shoulders convulsed with the effort to control his emotions.

"I've lost my job because of my farming. I've lost my wife and kids, my dignity, my future. I'm so far in debt I can't get out. When I heard that wheat went to $2.85 a bushel I lost hope. I've nowhere to turn."

At this he bowed his head and stood looking at the floor, beaten and worn down by a terrible addiction he had no way to control. There were no hospitals or treatment centers he could turn to for help. The United Farmer's Anonymous group held for him, his only hope.

The Wheel

Children's toys nowadays are getting out of hand. Just the other day I saw a toy advertised for ages three and up and it was priced just over two thousand dollars. My first tongue-in-cheek thought was "How can a modern child face his peers if he shows up with a hand made toy or worse yet a hand-me-down toy, or, heaven forbid, a broken or well used toy?" Surely a thinking parent would not give such an expensive toy to a child and risk warping a child's view of the value of toys. Toys are playthings of little or no value and should be the catalyst of thought and imagination, not some monetary investment that children will fight over because of its resale value.

I have watched my son play video games that leave no room for imagination. All the graphics are there and all you have to do is sit and look at a screen and wiggle your thumb at the right time. There is no question that they are fun, but kids nowadays have no appreciation for the power and overwhelming wonder of a well-tuned imagination.

My grandfather made me a toy when I was very small, that when compared with the toys of today appears foolish and very simple. But combined with an active imagination, it was as good a toy as any and I defy anyone to say that I had less fun with my toys than kids today have with theirs.

When I was young, thread came on a spool that was made of wood. My grandpa took one, and with his pocket knife carved a groove straight across the end about the width of the diameter of the centre hole and about an eighth of an inch deep. Next, he took a rubber band and fed it through the centre of the spool. A small stick that just fit the groove was slipped through one end of the rubber band and the band pulled from the opposite end to pull the little stick into the groove. A pencil sized stick was put through the rubber band at the other end of the spool. The larger stick was turned to wind up the rubber band and with a little soap as a lubricant between stick and spool it was placed on the floor and turned loose. The rubber band would unwind and the spool would roll across the floor pulling the big stick with it.

Grandpa would carve little notches around the edges of the spool to give it a little more traction and it would climb through carpet or across the furniture. We called it a tractor and it was the first self-propelled toy I'd ever seen. The tighter the band was wound the faster it would go. As the soap lubricant wore off, it would travel slower but the distance it went did not change much. With minor adjustments we could make it travel fast or slow. Before too long we could make our own, and soon all of Grandma's spools were spinning across the floor in races, climbing competitions and pulling contests.

With the principles learned, we made other homemade wind up toys – winches that would pull sticks in the sand box and catapults that could throw rocks across the yard towards Mum's windows.

Another simple toy was created with two feet of string and a large coat button. The thread was fed through one button hole and back through the other; the two ends were tied together creating a loop at both ends with the button in the middle. The button was spun and as a person alternately pulled and released the looped ends, the button would spin first one direction and then the other. With very little practice one could get the button spinning so fast that it would create a howling noise, at which point one would hold the spinning button close to one's Aunty Marian's hair, providing hours of entertainment watching Grandma trying to untangle it.

Grandpa had also built a marble track. It was about eighteen inches high and had a zigzag track running from the top to the bottom. One would drop a marble in the top corner and watch as the marble rolled one way and as it reached the end of the first track it would drop down to the next level and roll the other way, back and forth until it reached the bottom. Several marbles dropped in as fast as possible created traffic jams and pile-ups. We played for hours with it.

But I have told you only of the inside toys we had. Outside was where we spent all our time unless it was raining or cold enough that Mum would keep us in. Outside was where the fun really was. At Grandma's house we had the most wonderful things to play on. The most popular was the inner tube. It was originally inside an earthmover's tire. When blown up it was eight feet in diameter. Laying on the ground, it was almost two feet high. It became a trampoline, a raft on the swimming hole, a fifteen person toboggan hill inner tube, a fort for snowball fights, and we rolled down the hill inside it. Mostly it was a trampoline. One kid jumping on it was fun but as soon as there was more than one it became an insurmountable challenge to stay on it. As one person landed, it propelled whoever was opposite straight up, but only if they were exactly on the top. It would launch them straight out if they happened to be just off center or off balance when the other person jumped. It was a real accomplishment if you could bounce more than a few times without landing on the ground.

Uncle Ed could bounce me on the big tube higher than anyone else could and when someone as big as Ed went down, someone as big as me went way up. If you went straight up it was fun because you came straight down onto the tube, but if you were on the edge of it too much when you started out, you didn't go straight up, which presented a problem because the tube stayed where it was and you would come down onto the ground. A person can fall quite a ways and not get hurt. In fact, the falling doesn't hurt at all, it's the sudden stop at the end that hurts.

The amount of air in the tube made a difference, too. If it was pumped up tight it was more fun to just jump on it like a trampoline, but if it was half flat and someone else was jumping with you, it would shoot you quite a bit higher if the other person timed his jump just right. Ed was good at that.

I remember most of one time when he was bouncing me. I went straight up and came down straddling the tube. The next time I came down, I hit the tube on my back as he jumped again. I felt that I was almost in orbit.

When I regained consciousness, I was lying on the living room couch with Kay leaning over me saying, "Yup. He's breathing again."

I wasn't the only one to have that much fun on the tube. We always seemed to enjoy ourselves on it until someone had to be carried into the house, then the fun ended. But whenever I fell off and was feeling blue, I would just start breathing again and everything would be fine.

We took it to a tubing party on Stonehocker's Hill. It took more people to carry it up the hill than what could fit on it for the ride down, but we still managed to hurt Opal pretty good when she fell off into the center of the tube and was stuck in there bouncing along on the ground all the way to the bottom of the hill.

We took it to French Bay and it would float with fifteen or twenty kids on it but it was impossible to climb back on once Marian had pushed you off, and so you had to go back to the shore and sit on the beach and miss out on all the fun everyone else was having just because you were too short to get back on with out help, and nobody felt sorry for you and helped you. But I digress.

Another toy that Grandma had at her house was a merry-go-round. It was no ordinary merry-go-round, certainly not one of these wussy kind that are only six inches off the ground. This one was mounted on the top of a telephone pole that had been planted in Grandma's backyard. The bottom of it was about fifteen feet off the ground. It had four ropes hanging from it. Two of them, opposite one another, had a seat at the bottom a foot or so off the ground. The other two were just large ropes with a knot at the end. The intended victim – I mean, the small kid – would sit in one of the seats and the bigger kid would pull on the other ropes, spinning the merry-go-round. As the speed increased, centrifugal force would take the little kid higher and higher until he was screaming his heart out and begging and pleading with Uncle Ed to slow down and let him get off. There were times when I was sure the rope would break and I would be sent into orbit. It was wonderful fun.

Because of all the toys that were at Grandma's house, we all learned valuable skills, unlike the child of today who sits in front of a computer and hasn't learned even the basics of CPR or the rudimentary skills of splinting or controlling a hemorrhage.

Sandbox toys were also educational. We had a variety of sticks, a hook from a logger's cant hook, (see 'How To Wear Out a Washing Machine') and even a few store-bought trucks and tractors. But the most wonderful of all the toys I ever had was The Wheel. A wheel, I might add, that Heath full well knows the sentimental value of to me, but still refuses to give it back to the rightful owner and keeps it hidden away where his unappreciative kids are probably going to play with it and lose it, while my children, who are the rightful heirs, have spent their childhoods wheel-deprived.

The Wheel was, or is, four inches in diameter, one inch wide and has tractor tire tread on it. It is solid rubber except for the center hole where it used to fit onto some toy that Uncle Lloyd had as a kid. With a little imagination to fill in the missing parts, it became a tractor or a skidder or any variety of machines, but mostly it was a skidder.

Dad owned and operated a sawmill-logging business for many years and the skidder was the most fascinating machine there was. It could go through or over virtually anything. A skidder is a four wheel drive tractor specially designed for dragging logs out of the bush. A skidder works exclusively in the forest dragging the cut trees over stumps, logs, etc. and as a result, the tires of a skidder take a tremendous beating. Any skidder tire that has seen even a few hours of service will have chunks of rubber ripped out and tore off by the sharp sticks, and stumps. I had both ridden on and driven Dad's skidder before my sandbox career ended, and because the wear and tear the real tires were taking was such a fascinating thing for me to watch, that fascination was transferred to the sandbox.

 The Wheel, when gripped in one hand and rolled along on the ground one half a rotation at a time, would leave tracks in the sand that looked exactly like the skidder's tracks. There was a problem, though. If the sand was too dry, it left no tracks at all and then we had to play in the dirt of the garden where The Wheel would leave better tracks. Sticks and rocks were employed to drive The Wheel over. As The Wheel was rolled up against a stick it would compress and bulge exactly like a real tire did when driving over a stump or log, and when it was spun repeatedly on a rock or stick, small chunks of rubber began to be tore off until it looked like a perfect replica of a real skidder tire. It was thrilling. There is nothing to compare with the fun of holding that Wheel and rolling it back and forth over a stick.

 Heath and Nathan both knew what The Wheel meant to me and yet, when I left home and got married, they took it. I never realized it was missing until after my honeymoon and when I looked for it, it was not to be found. I was devastated by the loss, but as they say, time heals all wounds.

 Just a few years ago when I thought the hurt was gone, and when my youngest son was already in his teens, Heath confessed to the treachery of having in his possession The Wheel. His callous and unrepentant attitude when I told him how my own son has suffered through his youth Wheel-less is unforgivable. Not only that but Nathan claims The Wheel for himself and his posterity, and has sworn to avenge the perceived wrong unless Heath gives him The Wheel. I was mortified that he would even assume he had a claim upon the heirloom when it was so clearly mine. Neither one of them understands its true value, and are acting very childish about the whole matter. They should do the right thing and give it back. After all, I had it first.

Money won't buy happiness,
but it will buy all the things
I enjoy being miserable with.

*T*he *C*hefs

Uncle Jim taught me how to cook. We had decided to make lemon meringue pie which we figured would be pretty easy since all the ingredients were in the little box and the instructions were boldly printed on the side of the box. We had to wait until Grandma was gone somewhere so we wouldn't have to ask permission. She never seemed pleased to see us in her kitchen for some reason that I could never figure out. I know that the egg carton full of frogs in the fridge bothered her a little because it was one of only two occasions she ever gave me a lickin'. She didn't want to hear about our hibernation experiment. But other than that I don't recall anything we could have done to make her mistrust us.

Grandma had gone to Edmonton for the weekend. Jim and I had been left with the responsibility of making life as tough as possible for Kay and Marian. So after they had been sent off crying and whining over some imagined hurt, we headed for the kitchen to bake our pie.

Step one was to empty the contents of the box into a bowl.

"Man, this is going to be harder than we thought, eh?" Jim asked, as we swept the contents off the counter into a larger bowl.

Then came the hard part, adding a measured amount of water to the bowl.

When we were done the kitchen looked like a herd of pigs had been through there, except not quite so clean, but the pie actually looked okay and we were ready to bake it. The only problem was that the meringue on top was pure white. On every lemon pie we'd ever seen, the meringue had little brown tips on the swirls. We could not think what we could have left out. There must be something that will make the little swirls brown, but we could not figure out what it could possibly be. Then Jim had an epiphany.

"Pepper is brown. It's simply a matter of adding some pepper."

So we did. It took several tablespoons of pepper before we could see any change in the color, and the pepper wasn't accumulating at the swirl's tips the way it was supposed to. But being as humble as we were, we knew we couldn't expect perfection on the first try, so into the oven it went.

Thirty minutes later we had the best looking pie we'd ever baked. Being the gracious hosts that we were, we insisted that Kay and Marian have a piece. Oh, the whining and protest. You would think we were trying to poison them. We were persuasive, though, and in the end they tried some.

Not much of it was actually swallowed. To this day we have never figured out what we'd done wrong to make it taste so horrible. I figure whoever wrote the instructions on the box failed to anticipate chefs of our calibre and neglected to include some vital instruction.

The Dump

So, I went down to the dump the other day, and I'm like anyone else and had to look around and see what had been chucked out. It amazes me what people throw out sometimes. There was mostly just all kinds of trash, but occasionally you find something of value.

Anyway, I spotted what looked to be a bucket of Kentucky Fried Chicken down at the bottom of the pit so I climbed down to check it out and sure enough, there was a few pieces left that still had some meat on them. They look like they'd only been there for a couple days so I ate one. It was pretty good still so I started on another piece.

I'd just got nicely started when I saw Dave coming. He lived across the river from me but I know him quite well, and I didn't really want him to catch me down there eating chicken, so I jumped behind this old mattress that was half buried in the sludge at the bottom and in doing so stepped right in an old used diaper. It was one of those times when I wished I was wearing shoes.

So there I was crouched down behind an old mattress with an old piece of chicken, ankle deep in a black slimy sludge water soup with a bug crawling up my leg, hiding from Dave, who I happen to know is a bigger scavenger than I'll ever be.

I've seen him drinking the pop and beer left in the bottom of old cans, and stopping on the side of the highway to see if road kill was fresh enough to carry home to feed his young 'uns.

Anyway, the more I though about it, the madder I got. I have as much right to be there as he does, I don't care what he thinks, and besides, I was getting a real cramp in my back and that bug was already up to my thigh.

So I stood up. Dave just kind of stared at me with this blank look on his face, then walked over and grabbed my pieced of chicken. I was so shocked I just stood there and watched him eat it. I mean, what could I do? He out weighs me by more than a pound. But it still irks me something fierce the way ravens think they can just take what they want just cause they're bigger than us seagulls. It's just not fair. And besides, I had the chicken first.

The Dump Song

*To be sung in slow 12 bar blues time,
with the first line of each stanza repeated.*

My Woman up and left me way back when. 2x
So I've been living here in this dumpster since then.

A pair of head lights came along late one night. 2x
So I jumped back in the dumpster out of sight.

I learned you got to look before you jump. 2x
It was a garbage truck and I wound up at the dump.

> *Chorus*
> I'm down in the dumps but man I'm feelin' good. 2x
> I'm finally living free and eatin' like I should.

I'm eatin' free cause I'm living in a big buffet. 2x
I just make sure I don't eat nothin' grey.

That the food's gone bad is just a pack o' lies. 2x
All I gotta do is scrape away the flies.

The seagulls are always stealing what's rightly mine. 2x
I gotta fight 'em off even when I dine.

> *Chorus*

I found a new wardrobe but the underwear's way too tight. 2x
I sleep all day and I come out late at night.

I wear a three piece suit – says Armani on the tag. 2x
Oh, the treasure you find when you sort through every bag.

The sky's my roof and my bed is a cardboard box. 2x
I go barefoot so I don't change my socks.

    Chorus

Pop is free, I drink all that I can stand. 2x
There's a little bit left in the bottom of every can.

I had a pet skunk but as near as I can tell. 2x
I think he left me too cause he could not stand the smell.

A lot of people visit but they don't stay too long. 2x
When I invite them in they run like something's wrong.

    Chorus

*H*air *C*ut

*M*y wife cuts my hair. She says she does this to save money, as does your wife. This essay is written to expose the truth of these exaggerated claims. Money has no more to do with this marital exercise than divorce lawyers have with "peace and good will toward men."

This is the one time in every marriage when a husband is completely and utterly at her mercy, totally defenceless, and she takes full advantage of the situation to extract payment for all the real or perceived slights he has given her since the last haircut.

This, however, is not the primary reason. This is a practice which has been handed down since time immemorial. Not only is she getting revenge, but she is marking him as her property. Just as the cowboy chokes the young calf into submission with his lariat, then hogties it, and with a white hot iron burns through its hair and sears the skins below to mark it before the world that the calf is his, so too the woman places her mark on her husband. Any single girl can tell with a glance at his hair that he is a married man.

The man, however, submits to this to prove his unconditional faith and trust in his mate. Trusting her to bear and raise his children is one thing, but to show trust on an infinitely higher plain requires a haircut.

He is also proving his manhood, his nerves of steel. The young native of ages past would tie himself to tall poles with cords run through the skin of his chest which he had pierced with sharp bones. As he leaned his weight against the cords, the bones would pull free tearing through the skin as the young man danced and chanted. If he could bear this without complaint he was considered a man.

In a like manner and for the same reasons, the married man in silence allows his wife to cut his hair. If he would go to a modern hair salon he would place himself in the chair, at ease in the knowledge that the barber or hair dresser has been trained in a government sanctioned and inspected college for one, two or more years. They have been taught, trained, tested and corrected by competent professionals, emerging with a certificate announcing to the world that they possess the skill to shape and sculpt the hair to any desired shape or style.

In the salon the '*artiste de cheveux*' has at her fingertips electric trimmers, clippers, razors, elevating chairs, curlers, tongs, shampooers, rinsers, sinks, dryers, brushes arranged by bristle density, combs to straighten, combs to curl, and scissors to cut, trim, thin, eradicate or lengthen any color hair you may have.

My wife has a comb, electric clippers and a set of pruning shears hanging in the garden shed that she refers to as scissors.

"How hard can it be?" she asks, feigning innocence and fluttering her eyelashes.

I sit in the chair.

She ties a towel around my neck. This is to soak up the blood. She then takes a squirt bottle that she had stored in the refrigerator and squirts me once in the eye and three times in my left ear. She takes the shears in both hands and cuts a diagonal line through the hair on my forehead.

"This is a gauge," she informs me. It shows her what length the hair should be once it grows back.

The comb is then employed and is dragged through the hair directly opposite to the direction the hair lays. She is able to do this by grasping the comb with both hands, placing her knee between my shoulder blades for leverage, then jerking the comb repeatedly until it comes free.

This is referred to as 'thinning.'

The shears are brought to bear again and attacks are made against the survivors of the thinning, with only a tuft here or there escaping untouched.

"It's a good thing your hair is curly," she remarks. "It hides any irregularities."

She then trims around the ears, being careful not to cut the ear in the same spot as last time as the scar is not fully healed.

"Here, just use the corner of the towel. Hold it right there. That's right. It'll quit in a minute."

I press the towel to my ear. My children enter the room to inquire about the commotion. She sarcastically tells them I was criticizing her barber skills.

She turns back to me and snaps, "Other side now!" By placing her left thumb in my right eye socket she is able to jerk my head to the right eighty degrees, traumatizing the spinal cord and exposing the jugular. She slashes wildly at me with the shears and my sideburns disappear.

"Oops. Don't worry. I'll just do the other side again a little bit. I like them a little shorter anyway."

Once the sideburns match she goes to the medicine cabinet and retrieves a band aid. She comes back with it, and with the scissors, gives me a deep gash at the base of the neck and puts the band aid on it.

"You have a bald spot," she informs me.

"Where?" I ask.

She takes the scissors and trims away all the hair to reveal it.

"Right there," she says. "You're getting grey, too. One little trim in the back and we're done. I'll get the clippers."

She rummages through the cupboard drawer and pulls out a set of electric clippers, plugs them in and flips the switch on. They begin to buzz like a kicked wasp nest. Then taking a run from the far side of the room, she drives the clippers into the base of my neck. As the clippers labour to cut through both hair and skin, she leans on them with her free hand. This allows her to take another full inch of hair after the clippers stall completely. With a twist and yank they come free and she wipes them on the towel. One more run at it and she pronounces me finished, and I am.

I make a break for it and hide in the shower until the adrenalin subsides.

As I think about it I come to the conclusion that if I would have gone to a professional, they would have charged me twenty dollars but I got a two dollar haircut at home for free.

The Moskeeter

The moskeeter is a game bug but it won't bite at a hook. Still, there's millions of them caught every year and this makes the market very unsteady as the supply exceeds the demand.

Moskeeters are born on the sly and come to maturity quicker than any other of the domestic animals. The moskeeter at three hours old is just as ready and willing to go into business for himself as he ever is, and he bites just as sharp and natural the first time as red pepper.

The moskeeter has a good ear for music and sings without notes. The song of the moskeeter is monotonous to some folks but in me it stirs up the memories of other days. Why, I've laid awake all night long many a time, listening to the sweet anthems of the moskeeter.

I'm satisfied there weren't nothing made in vain but I can't help thinking how close the moskeeter come to it.

Moskeeters have inhabited this world since the beginning and will probably be around when business closes. Where the moskeeter goes in the winter time is a standing conundrum which all the naturalists have give up. But we know he don't go far 'cause he's right there every spring with his proboscis buffed, ground and polished.

The moskeeter is one of the luxuries of life. They certainly ain't one of the necessaries.

My *C*hristmas *P*oem

By Kyla Hatch
(And Some Help From Her Dad)

T'was a month before Christmas
And all through the mall,
There were so many shoppers
Jammed in wall to wall.

In a credit card frenzy
Buying trinkets and trees,
Induced by commercials
They saw on T.V.

No will of their own,
No self discipline.
Pushing and shoving,
'Round the big bargain bin.

If it's on sale buy it,
No need to think twice.
I have my Visa,
Don't care 'bout the price.

I'm driven to purchase
To shop and to spend.
I buy it and charge it.
Oh, where will it end?

Now I'm overdrawn
Beyond all reason.
But I guess that's okay
Because it's the season.

I look at these shoppers
And what do I find?
All of them have
Just one thing on their mind.

And that thing is not
The miraculous birth,
Of Him who's the author
Of Peace on the Earth.

So maybe this year
Thru this Christmas season,
Please, let's remember
The real Christmas reason.

The Helper

The definition of mixed feelings
Is when my little guy
Says "Dad, I'm comin' to help ya!"
You either take him or make him cry.

Now, I love to have him with me.
There's no one I love more,
But it takes less time to do the job
Than to get him out the door.

He tries to get his boots on
And I just have to laugh.
"What you mean they're on the wrong feet?
They're the only feet I have."

I zip his coat then find his mitts
And his ski-doo suit for the snow.
I finally get him all dressed up
He says "Dad, I gotta go."

He helps me fix machinery.
I try not to get mad.
"I know that you are helpin'
But where's the wrench that I just had?"

The hammer's always easy to find.
He always leaves a trail.
On any handy surface
There's a row of little nails.

If you ask him he's helpin'
And in his little mind
He thinks if he's not helpin' Dad
His Dad just couldn't get by.

Now my favorite helper
Is the kid I call my son.
He helped me all day yesterday
But I got a fair bit done.

I've had many people help me
But as the years go by,
The helper I'll remember most
Will be my little guy.

*A M*an's *L*ife

When I was eight I became a man (I could sleep out in the woods).
Hafta be a man to sleep outside. And if your mother said you could,
From that day on it was no holds barred and I let the world know
That I could do most anything.
If it was alright with her, you know.

Some days I'd be a pirate on my raft down by the river,
A swash buckling buccaneer so tough it'd make you shiver.
I'd sail that raft around the world anywhere the wind would blow
And I wouldn't come home 'til after dark,
If it was alright with her, you know.

Some days I'd be a farmer driving tractor, cutting hay.
Sometimes I would decide that I would just stay home and play.
Some days I'd weed the garden if I'd nowhere else to go.
Some days I'd just go fishin',
If it was alright with her, you know.

At school I never had much luck, I couldn't learn my letters.
My teacher always told my Mum "That boy, he could do better."
I decided that a college was a place I would not go.
And that's just what I told my Mum,
If it was alright with her, you know.

Then one day I bought a truck and that's how freedom feels,
To cruise the town and look for chicks in a brand new set of wheels.
I could go here, I could go there, or to the drive-in picture show.
I might even take the neighbour girl,
If it's alright with her, you know.

Then one day I met a girl. I could tell she's meant for me.
But I knew I'd have to date her once so she could clearly see,
That I was a man of talent and skill with important places to go.
I decided then I'd date that girl,
If it's alright with her, you know.

She fell in love as I hoped she would, so then one clear spring day
I told her that I loved her too and I'd take her far away
To a beautiful land of forest and stream where wild flowers grow.
To a quaint little house by a beautiful lake,
If it's alright with her, you know.

I'm an independent, self made man endowed with great ability.
I do my job and I'm not afraid of manly responsibility.
Supporting my wife and children, is a difficult job I know.
But I always do what I know is best
If it's alright with her, you know.

I cut my hair the way I like, I dress the way I choose,
And if I'm feeling tired I just lay down for a snooze.
I'm independent and I love it. I may let my whiskers grow.
Yes, I do anything I want
If it's alright with her, you know.

Yes I like being married and my wife, she likes it too.
And if it's not presumptuous I'll give advice to you.
If you really love your wife then you should let her know
Hug and kiss her every day
If it's alright with her, you know.

I love my wife and I'll stick by her, forever, come what may.
I'll hold her hand and be her friend when she turns old and gray.
It doesn't matter what time does. There is one thing I know,
I'll stick by her forever more
If it's alright with her, you know.

This poem was written shortly after the birth of my daughter Kyla.

Little Girls

I think the Lord loves little girls.
He made each one with care,
With eyes and smiles to win your heart,
Round cheeks and soft brown hair.
Small pink hands that grasp your thumb
But won't reach all around.
So small you're afraid that she might break
But can't bear to put her down.
You only have to hold her once
Before you fall in love
And swear you'll take good care of her
And give her all you have.
Her eyes meet yours and then she smiles
That toothless little grin.
A devotion builds inside your heart
That kings could never win.

You slowly start to understand
The worth of that little girl,
Worth more than all the riches
Of this good for nothing world,
I sure love my little girl.
And I can finally see
How my father-in-law loves his little girl
And why he despises me.

*H*ayden

*H*ayden was born at a very young age on December 14, 1970 and kind of stayed that way. We had no idea what was in store for our family. We knew he was different and I suppose we were all a little scared of what was to come.

Hayden had Down's Syndrome. None of us knew what that meant. My mind went from visions of monsters to deformed people who drooled and stared into space. Mum asked me if we should keep him. The thinking in those days was that handicapped children should be taken away and kept from society in an institution. We decided to keep him. How wise that decision was.

Shortly after Hayden was born, a church leader, I don't recall who, told Mum that Hayden had been sent to our family to teach us things that we would never learn otherwise. What I do know to be true is that he did indeed have a tremendous effect on us and many other people, and taught us a lot of things. Hayden was the first handicapped person that many in our community had ever met, or at least the first that they had anything to do with. Hayden had a unique personality. It didn't matter who you were, Hayden loved you unconditionally whether you were old or young, but he got along really well with the little kids. Every woman or girl was, as he put it, "a beautiful woman." Everyone was immediately considered his bosom buddy. Hayden did not fake his love for anyone.

Any of those who knew him have heard him say, "Oh, lucky you." and he meant it. Our accomplishments made him happy for us. There was no envy.

He did have a great desire to have what we took for granted like getting married, going on a mission, singing, participating in discussions and storytelling, but he was genuinely glad for us and would tell us, "Lucky you."

I walked down the street in Grande Centre with Hayden one day and had people wave to him on the street and say, "Hi Hayden." Store owners, people on the sidewalk and an RCMP officer – I had lived there all my life and I didn't know who they were but they knew Hayden. I don't know why or how but he had obviously met them somewhere and had enough of an effect on them that they remembered who he was.

Hayden was a gifted child and so he started school at the age of three, and he provided no end of entertainment to everyone on the bus. Well, everyone except his siblings, who spent many miles with their heads hid under the seat. Hayden's imaginizer worked just fine and he would drape a rag or plastic bag over his hand and pretend it was a beautiful princess that he was in love with. Sometimes his romances with his rags would end with a passionate kiss. On one bus ride home he did not have a rag to play with but he did have a pair of underwear that he had wet at school and the teacher was sending home for Mum to wash out. When all the kids on the bus realized that Hayden had his dirty underwear on his hand and it was transforming into a princess, he had their undivided attention. I think all of us siblings had our heads hidden, but we could tell when the passionate kiss happened when every kid on the bus yelled eewww!

Hayden also suffered from undiagnosed diabetes for many years which made him extremely thirsty. He would literally drink gallons of water a day. As a result, his bladder became worthy of the bladder hall of fame. He very seldom made it all the way to school without stopping to pee somewhere along the bus route, and having a bladder that could provide a non-stop stream for three to four minutes was an added embarrassment to his siblings, especially when the students on the bus would start betting on how long he would go off the bus steps.

Hayden had one school teacher in particular who had a great impact on him and several other handicapped kids in the area. Her name was Hanna Siemonson. She treated Hayden and the others whom she taught differently than others might have. In her eyes they were people with great potential. She saw Hayden as having just as much value to our society as anyone else, and treated them as such. We all learned that she was right. I believe that Hayden has changed all of our attitudes toward any who are handicapped.

Hayden started school in 1973 and graduated in 1991. Graduation was his proudest achievement and he always talked about when he graduated. At his graduation, he got a new suit custom tailored and had grad pictures taken. To look at his picture you would think that if he smiled any harder he would blow a gasket. At the awards ceremony his name was called and he strutted up to receive his certificate. When he turned to walk back to his seat, the entire graduating class stood and gave him a standing ovation. He knew at that moment that he was just as wonderful and glamorous as he had thought he was. A whole bunch of the other kids and grads went to Hayden's place for a grad party. At one o'clock in the morning the party was going strong when Hayden stood up and announced, "Go home. I'm tired and going to bed." And then he started handing out coats. He could be very honest.

A couple of years ago, the high school Hayden attended sent a reporter out to interview some of the students who had graduated years before, to see where they were and what they were up to. Hayden was on the list. The reporter phoned Mum and asked to speak to Hayden. When she started to talk to Hayden, it was the first she knew that he was handicapped. No one had told her.

When Hayden was diagnosed with cancer, a group of Hayden's high school teachers sent him a card expressing their concern. There's not too many of us whose school teachers are still concerned about us, but Hayden's love for others was almost always reciprocated.

Hayden's personality was such that he would not stand in the background with his head down like an outcast. He wanted to be in the middle of whatever was happening and he pulled his friends in with him. He was not shy and at school dances had no qualms about asking the prettiest girls to dance with him, and they would. It became a status symbol to be asked by Hayden to dance because that meant that he thought you were beautiful. Nathan would go around after saying, "I'm Hayden's brother. Will you dance with me, too?"

Hayden knew there was nothing wrong with him. One day Heath and Nathan were giving him a hard time about something. Dad stepped in in Hayden's defence and said, "Give him a break, he's handicapped."

Hayden immediately turned on Dad and declared, "Me not handicapped. Me a retard."

He knew who he was and what made him different and was not ashamed of it. I heard him say on other occasions that he had a "thick brain" and a "thick tongue".

Oh how he wanted his tongue to work. To be able to sing was one of his greatest dreams and he would practice endless hours singing along with tapes of the Mormon Tabernacle Choir or Anne Murray, Abba or some Disney princess soundtrack. To us he sounded like a goat with bronchitis, but if you believe what the scriptures say about the value of a 'joyful noise unto the Lord', I guess we would have to class it as much music as many of us can produce.

Hayden's singing had always been interesting if not embarrassing. Hayden spent hours pretending that he was part of the Mormon Tabernacle Choir. He would put on a cassette tape of the choir and then sit and bray as the choir sang. He would not sing every word because he was just not fast enough so he would wait until the end of a phrase, and then upon hearing the last word of the phrase, he would bellow it out. It didn't matter if the choir was singing in the key of D or maybe G, Hayden was singing in H flat minor. He had managed to get a Suffolk-like vibrato in his voice that he had worked on for years, trying to sound like Merlene Hatch, who was an accomplished singer. The combined effect sounded like the Tabernacle Choir was providing backup music for some sort of pagan, sacrificial goat slaughter.

In Sunday School one day, he learned that after we die we will be resurrected with a perfect body, one that will have a heavenly voice. So a light went on in his mind, not a bright one, but a light nonetheless and Hayden's goal thereafter was to get himself resurrected. Then he would be able to sing like an angel. Trying to figure out how to be resurrected was where the logic began to fail a little bit. He knew that dying was a prerequisite for resurrection but he couldn't figure out how to accomplish it without hurting himself, or worse yet, leaving his mother. So the problem remained unsolved until the day his mother bought fifteen cases of green peaches.

They had been in BC and Mum had bought peaches, and seeing that it was a ten hour drive home they put the peaches in the back of their suburban covered with a blanket. Hayden rode in the back seat and on the way home he got hungry and decided to sneak a peach. He was able to do it without Mum seeing, and although it was a little green he ate it. Hayden has never been one to not eat just because the food didn't taste good. He would eat as long as there was food of any sort to be had. He soon realized that he was on to a good thing and the peaches just kept sneaking into his hand. As long as Mum didn't notice, he figured there would be no harm in eating a couple cases.

If a body eats ten or twenty pounds of green peaches, interesting things begin to happen. Things like chemical reactions that involve fermentation, toxic gases, high pressures and other related chain reactions that one learns about only too late. Luckily things reached critical mass after they had arrived home.

Now one has to realize two things at this point from Hayden's point of view. First, if one gets violently ill, it is a sure sign of imminent death. Secondly, death, remember, is a prerequisite for resurrection, which is what one wants if one needs an angelic voice. The problem, though, is even though the thoughts of dying are enough to make one ecstatically happy, the subsequent illness from the peaches tends to put a damper on the festivities.

Hayden was overjoyed with the fact that he felt so sick he was going to die. But just when he thought the end was near, the washroom suddenly had an overpowering attraction. In a few moments it wasn't the attraction that was overpowering.

But then........ a miracle! A cure!

In just a few minutes on the toilet, Hayden had suffered a miraculous cure. The pain was gone. He felt fine. Oh, what a disappointment. The suffering was over. All his hopes of an unpleasant death were dashed by a simple case of diarrhoea. The disappointment of being reprieved from certain death kept him in a blue funk for days.

Many of us leave our talents undeveloped because we think we are not as good as we should be and are afraid that some one might criticise us. We forget that to get good, we have to work at it. Hayden got as good as he could. He developed his talents to the fullest extent possible and there are not too many of us who can make that claim.

Once Hayden got an idea in his head, he was committed to it and changing his mind was not an easy task. He taught us that arguing with someone who knows less than you do is a pointless endeavour and I guess arguing with someone who knows more than you is pointless too. The only way to get Hayden to do what you wanted was to follow the way the Savior taught people.

First was to gain his respect by showing him that you loved him and then simply telling him what the rule was. Once he understood what the rule was he was glad to obey it.

One of Hayden's rules was that he was not allowed to watch TV until he had walked a mile on his "windmill" (treadmill). One morning he woke up to discover that Mum and Dad were not home. He had been told that they would be gone for several hours, but he had forgotten. So he walked a half mile down to Nathan's house to see if they were there. They weren't, so he phoned home and left a message on the phone for his mother, asking her where she was and telling her to hurry home. He then left Nathan's and walked home and checked the phone messages. He spent the rest of the day mad because he "no can't watch TV" because he was too tired to walk on the windmill. Breaking the rule never entered his mind.

Hayden had a love of the scriptures his whole life and studied them faithfully. He would spend hours copying them out or following along in his scriptures as he listened to them read on tape. In the last few months of his life, Hayden read the scriptures beginning with Genesis, chapter 1 and ending with the last chapter of the Pearl of Great Price. He did this more than once in his life and did it with a grade 2 reading ability. The recall mechanism wasn't working but the knowledge was stored, and when the time comes and his tongue is loosed I firmly believe that he will be able to teach the gospel like few others.

He had several callings in the church and took them very seriously. He loved to go home-teaching, and would phone whoever was his companion at the time, never letting them forget. He loved to conduct the music and over the last month or so was concerned over how we are going to get by without him to pick the hymns and lead the music. We would do well to have some of Hayden's testimony of and willingness to follow the Savior.

He taught us that flattery will get you everywhere. If he was invited over for dinner somewhere he would not ask for seconds. He would simply gaze longingly at the mashed potatoes and gravy and tell you how delicious they were and what a good cook you must be, until you asked if he would like some more.

He would then act surprised and say, "Oh yes, thack oo."

Hayden loved to eat, fried chicken if he had a choice, but anything would do in a pinch including the dog scraps. One day he was sent out to scrape the scraps off the plates after dinner. When he didn't come back in the house for awhile Mum went to see what he was up to and caught him eating the scraps himself while the dog sat there watching him. If he was invited over for dinner somewhere, as soon as he got home there would be a detailed, play-by-play account of what he had for supper.

Hayden could choose to be happy. It was the most bizarre thing to watch. Many times he would be crabby, miserable and hard to live with until finally, when Mum was at her breaking point she would say, "Do you want me to get the happy stick?" Hayden would make a 180 degree attitude change and be happy, not a put on façade to try and placate you, but he would actually become happy. Happiness is a choice and if Hayden could do it I suppose we should be able to, too.

Hayden had a friend growing up whom he worshiped, one friend who always loved him and invited him over for dinner and made him feel like he was important. That friend was his "Uncle Yim."

Every Sunday morning when we lived in Cherry Grove, Hayden would "ax my Mum me go Yim house eat dinner?"

Yim could do no wrong in his eyes. Riding on Jim's bus was a thrill. Staying over at Jim's house was an occasion that needed to be marked on the calendar and each day meticulously x'ed out as the day approached, just as he did at Christmas or important birthdays.

Mum, like almost every other parent, has always had a hard time with her kids growing up too fast. All of us who have been parents have marvelled at how fast time goes, and we wish that our child would stay small and cute forever. Mum got her wish with Hayden. It is not something to wish for. As wonderful as small children are, we learned that we want our children to grow up, to progress and learn new things. Hayden grew and progressed 'til he was about four, and then hit a plateau. If you look at his school pictures you cannot tell the chronological order of the pictures.

Be glad that your children change and grow up. The 'terrible twos' don't last forever. Be grateful that you have the opportunity to see them learn about their fascinating world. Be thankful for the teenage years as they discover that they are smarter than every one else in the world, and won't take your advice. It is part of the progression of life. Be grateful that you can watch them grow.

We moved into the river house at Cherry Grove just about the time that Hayden started school. The driveway was about a third of a mile long and for years was impassable if it rained or snowed and drifted in. When that happened, we walked out to the bus and home from the road. I carried Hayden down that road many times and as I did I would jokingly sing the song, "He Ain't Heavy, He's My Brother." It wasn't until years later that I actually knew the words to that song and when I did, it started to have a whole new meaning for me. Especially the lines about caring for our brother and how the road is long but we can get there if we help and love one another.

All those who loved Hayden have carried him in one way or another. There were very few things that he could do for himself, and he needed to be carried and helped along by all those who cared for and loved him. Sometimes when we are struggling under a burden we look at nothing but the ground and we miss the scenery around us and fail to notice the strength we are gaining from our struggles. Sometimes the road we are on seems all uphill and sometimes with Hayden it was uphill for years at a time. We have all carried him many times and his five brothers and nephew had, as pallbearers, the honour of carrying him one more time to where his imperfect body will wait while his perfect spirit rests from the difficulties he had here.

We have come to the end of the road and have reached the top of the climb with him. I look back now and see the beautiful view of life that Hayden has given me from here, and I look forward to the time when I can meet him again and listen to the angelic singing voice I'm sure the Lord has given him. I'm sure he earned it.

Life is a mirror: if you frown at it, it frowns back; if you smile, it returns the greeting.
— William Makepeace Thackeray

The Little House

My earliest memories take place in the 'little house'. The little house was built by my grandpa's brother Darnell. Dad and Mum bought it from Uncle Darnell and were living there when I was born, so I decided to live there, too.

The outside measurements were twenty feet by twenty feet. Once the furniture was in, it seemed as though the measurements were eight by twelve.

The house was divided into three rooms. The living room took up the south half. The north half of the house was split into a bedroom and a kitchen. The bedroom was about eight by eight with almost enough room to put a double bed and a small dresser.

The kitchen was about the same size as the bedroom and had a small counter, a table and an old wood fired cook stove that Mum had scrounged when the museum had chucked it out. Apparently it was too old for them to be interested in it.

At one end of the living room was a double bed where Heath, Nathan and Hayden slept. At the foot of that bed was a wooden framed bunk bed that Grandpa Pollock had made just for me. I was gracious enough to share it with Shelby. She slept on the bottom and I on the top. At the foot of the bunk bed was Mum's chesterfield. A desk was squeezed in between the chesterfield and the wall at the far end. This pretty well filled every available space except for a four foot wide trail that led from the kitchen to the bedroom.

Right in the middle of the house at the junction of the walls that separated the rooms was a hole in the floor about eighteen inches square, covered with a heavy steel screen. Directly beneath that hole was a dirt floored basement that was home to countless unnamed monsters and other horrors. One of those horrors was a diesel furnace that coughed and roared and made other scary noises right below the screen.

It was an idyllic little cottage with none of the expensive paraphernalia that encumbers modern homes. There was no indoor plumbing of any sort to plug up or back up. No telephone for nosy neighbors or friends to pester you with, interrupting your solitude. No television, either, with its corrupting influence on the children. We had a sandbox to play in outside and almost unlimited space in the bush and fields that surrounded the house.

Mum went away to visit her mother, Grandma Pollock, one summer. I don't remember why I stayed home but I was thrilled to stay with Dad because we had a surprise for Mum when she got home. It was pretty fun to be in on the secret. Uncle Jim and Uncle Ed and I think Uncle Byron came down to our place and helped us dig a well.

We went straight west from the house about one hundred fifty yards into the bush and they started to dig. It was exciting to watch the hole getting deeper and deeper. One guy would be in the hole filling a five gallon pail with dirt and the other guys would hoist the full buckets up with a rope and empty them. When the hole was about fifteen feet deep they hit water and Dad built a well cribbing with 2x8's.

Talk about your modern conveniences. I couldn't wait for Mum to get home. When she did I could hardly contain myself.

"Mum! Come on! Let me show you." I grabbed her hand and led her down the trail to the well. "Look at this, Mum. All you have to do is let the bucket down like this with this rope and when you pull it back up it's full of water. Then all you have to do is carry the bucket back to the house. Pretty cool, eh?"

Mum was so thrilled there were tears in her eyes. The novelty wore off about a month later when a muskrat fell in and died. The water started to get a tangy taste to it, and the day we let down the bucket and the source of the flavor surfaced, so did Mum's tears. We went back to hauling water from a spring down by the river at Grandpa Hatch's old homestead site.

By the next year, the well cribbing had caved in. From then on, the well only produced entertainment by providing a place for small boys to drop things in and listen to the splash. I'm sure if an archeologist dug up that well he would never be able to explain why there would be such a variety of artifacts there. Many's the time that Dad accused me of losing his tools, but I knew exactly where they were. He just never asked.

The next well was tried in the basement. I wasn't sure if that was a good idea or not. No one had asked my opinion on it. Mum had told me to never go near the trap door in the pantry, so I knew that there must be terrible dangers there, and here was Ed and Dad OPENING the trap door and… and…and…CLIMBING DOWN INTO THE HOLE!!! I was terrified that they would never be seen again. I could hear their voices and they didn't seem scared, and in a minute up came a bucket of dirt. Jim hauled it outside and dumped it. Mum held my hand and let me venture just close enough to look down to where Dad and Ed were digging a hole in the dirt floor of the basement right at the bottom of the ladder.

They weren't much deeper than Ed's head when I heard Ed say, "I've hit quicksand."

I'd heard about quicksand before and my heart began thumping. I knew that Uncle Ed was a goner.

"Good," said my Dad, in the most callously calm voice. Didn't he know that Ed was in mortal peril, about to be sucked down to oblivion with nothing left but his pith helmet floating on the surface as the painted cannonballs chanted and danced around the perimeter of the quicksand?

I'd seen it happen on a movie at Grandma Pollock's house. In the movie, an explorer was running through the jungle being chased by bloodthirsty cannonballs who were throwing spears at him and Grandma had said that if the quicksand hadn't got him the cannonballs would have caught him and eaten him anyway. Movies with cannonballs that eat people and quicksand should never be watched by five year old boys, because after the well was covered, Dad built stairs that went right over top of that well and I had to jump the last three steps to avoid being grabbed by a cannonball that might be hiding in the quicksand under the stairs.

I heard them talking about a 'sandpoint' which I later learned was a pointy pipe with holes in it that was pushed down into the sand far enough so that Uncle Ed could pound it with a hammer and damage the threads. Then another pipe goes from that one to the pump. The pump had a hole in the top where Dad poured in water to 'prime the pump.' I was watching the whole procedure and could see that meant filling the well, because they would pour in five gallons, run the pump for a minute, pour in another five, run the pump, pour in another five, etc., etc. I looked down the well and sure enough, the well was filling up. If Jim and Ed would just haul the water a little faster they would have the well filled in no time at all, but it took them days hauling from the spring before the well was primed. You should have seen the look on Mum's face, though, when they got it going and more than two quarts of the prettiest brown water came out of the tap.

I thought it wasn't fair when Mum told Dad, "You can bath in it."

and then she took us to Grandma Hatch's and made us bath there, missing out on the first bath in the little house.

Before too many years had passed, Mum grew tired of having so much room upstairs and she began mixing cement in a wheel barrow in the basement. It didn't take more than a few months of hauling cement and gravel into the house in five gallon pails before she had the basement floor covered with cement and us kids' beds moved downstairs. Hayden still slept upstairs. Heathen Nathan slept on my wooden bunk beds and Shelby and I got a new steel framed bunk bed. It was made of angle iron with a web of wires under the mattress. Shelby slept on the bottom and I slept on top. At least I slept as long as Shelby wasn't bothering me and tormenting me by putting her feet against the bottom of my bed and pushing up my mattress. She would sometimes be kicking me so hard that my mattress would be bouncing a foot or more off the springs.

One night Mum came down to tuck us in like she normally did and she tucked the blankets right in tight against me, pinning my arms to my sides. As soon as Mum had gone upstairs Shelby began kicking the bottom of my bed. I rolled over as far as my pinned arms would allow so that I could politely ask her to stop. (I was always the epitome of politeness and courteousness.) As I did so she timed her next kick (deliberately, I might add) so that my entire mattress flipped off the bed and fell onto the concrete floor with me under it. My arms were pinned to my sides by the blankets the whole time and time seemed to slow down as I saw the concrete floor rushing up to meet my nose. It would prove to be the first of many times where my siblings were to be the cause of my undeserved suffering.

It was a wonderful house full of all kinds of things to entertain small children. When it rained, Mum could catch water in the rain barrels and in pots right inside the house. Talk about convenience. In the summertime we used an outhouse. If it was dark Mum would just walk out there with us so the coyotes and boogey men couldn't get us, and she would stand outside the door of the outhouse yelling, "Yes I'm still here!" and "We don't have any. Just use a page from the catalogue!"

In the winter we didn't even have to go out to the outhouse. We had a five gallon pail in the porch that Mum could just haul out and empty when it got full. With five kids and all of these conveniences, Mum could hardly keep up. As a matter of fact I saw her one day while she was hanging washed diapers on the clothes line and she paused and gazed at the house with kind of a wistful look for a few minutes and sighed. I could tell she was content.

One day we were in the house and there was a puff of smoke, a whooshing sound and flame about three feet high shot through the screen in the floor. The diesel furnace had blown up and flames were licking at the floor all around the screen. Mum stood and looked at it for a minute.

"Let's go outside," she said.

We all trooped outside.

"Everybody stand here and don't move," Mum directed.

So we stood there as Mum hurried back into the house and came back out carrying a stack of photo albums. She set them down and walked around to the side of the house and opened the valve on the fuel tank, and then kicked in the basement windows.

"Why did you do that, Mum?"

"So the fire will have enough air. Let's go get Dad."

So we all started walking out to the field to get Dad. Along the way Mum stopped to show us some flowers that were still in bloom, I think they were tiger lilies. They have always been my favorites and Mum told us they were hers, too. We saw some birds and other things too as we walked along the trail that led through the bush to the field. Hayden had to stop and take a leak for awhile. When we got to the field, Dad was on the far end so we sat down in the shade to wait for him. We watched as the tractor was chugging away, getting closer and closer. Finally he got to where we were waiting.

"What's up?" he called.

"The house is on fire," Mum said, not bothering to get up from where she was sitting in the shade.

Dad's eyes bugged out for a second and then he leaped from the tractor. His legs were in high gear before he hit the ground and he shot back down the trail like an Olympic sprinter, his cowboy boots shooting out a cloud of dust with each stride. Mum got up and we followed her back to the house.

Dad was standing in the middle of the yard just looking at the house. It didn't look any different to me, other than the windows were so black you couldn't see in. We went in. The windows were still so black you couldn't see out. In fact everything was black. It was so cool. We could draw pictures with our fingers in the soot everywhere. In seconds we were having a great time and Mum didn't even stop us. I think she'd gone for another walk or something, she didn't seem very happy, and was really crabby for the next few days while she was hauling water and washing everything.

I never remember the house being cold but after that day, try as she might, Mum would always complain that she couldn't get the furnace burning properly again.

Mum had a garden that was at least nine hundred acres. It may not have looked that large to the average person but just let that average person be five years old and charged with weeding two or three rows of it and they would think that nine hundred acres is a conservative estimate. In fact, my mother could think of nothing else that would be more fun for children to do than to weed the garden. We spent many of the carefree years of our childhood enjoying the thrills and delights of horticulture. When we finally moved to the big house by the river Mum was able to increase the size of her garden to just under two thousand acres. That may be a slight exaggeration, but I have never heard my mother say that the weeding was done. She may have said that we had done enough for the day but it was never done.

One day Mum found a house stuck out in the middle of a farmer's field north of Bonnyville that had been built in the late Jurassic period. It had been abandoned for many years and the mice had moved in. It had no power, no plumbing and no insulation but it had room. It had four huge bedrooms upstairs and one downstairs, a kitchen, a dining room and a big living room. The price was $500. Mum put a mortgage on three of the children and bought it.

Mum and Dad knew the perfect spot to put it. One mile south of the little house was a meadow on the crest of the river valley where you could see for miles down the valley in either direction. They had this house site picked out years before. We had had picnics on that spot before and we would sit gazing out at the river valley and dream, and now Mum's dreams were to come true – a real house on the most picturesque site I have ever seen.

For the next year we worked getting ready to move it home. We had to cut the porches off and cut the top of the roof off so that it would fit under the power lines. We dug a basement and built cinderblock walls. At last the day came to move the house. Dad was afraid that if he tried to move such a big house that far he would drop it and wreck it so he hired a professional crew that was able to do it for him. The house wound up on its corner in the bottom of the basement hole. It was such a well built house, though, that they didn't even break a window.

Once it was lifted back out of the hole and was on the basement, we moved in. We couldn't wait and didn't care if there were no doors or stairs to get in. It took a couple years to get the house wired for electricity and to get some plumbing in, but we had room, glorious room.

I have a picture of myself at sixteen, bathing in a round wash tub.

My siblings had burst in on me to get a photographic record of the last bath in the wash tub. Plumbing was only days away. I was thrilled that they would include me in their celebrations in such a way.

The furnace was an insatiable monster and it seemed as though I did nothing but chop wood all winter to feed it. My room upstairs never did have heat in it and on the coldest winter days a glass of water would freeze on my dresser if I left my door closed. That was a small price to pay for having a room all to myself.

I never saw that house finished. All the years I lived in it, it was one long continuous renovation project. When I left home at nineteen, the original asphalt siding was still on in most spots, the shiplap lumber that sheeted it underneath showed in many places. Mum and Dad had spent all their time and money to put in bathrooms, insulation, wiring, drywall, paint and wallpaper.

The house looked pretty shabby on the outside, but the inside was full of people who loved each other, full of the sounds of kids playing at the top of their lungs, full of Christmas parties that consisted of half of the population of Cherry Grove. It was decorated with tears and smiles, bandages and blood, refurbished furniture and Christmas trees. The door jambs were marked forever where small boys pretended that Mum's butcher knife was a machete and they were hacking their way through the jungle.
It was filled at times with the sound of sibling rivalries and squabbles but it was very seldom polluted with television or newspapers.

I went back there a couple of years ago and the little house is still struggling to stand. Its roof is caving in and in a few years it will be nothing more than a hole in the ground filled with rotting wood. The 'River House' as we called it is gone. Someone with no sentimental attachment to it burned it down and moved in a new manufactured home. When I first saw it was gone, a wave of nostalgia washed over me bringing me almost to tears and then the thought hit me.

Who needs reality? Those houses, and all who helped fill them with memories, still stand in my memory and always will.

Why does reality have such a warped view of me? It's because I don't need money to be rich. I've learned we don't need a life filled with pleasure to be happy. Life is one exciting adventure to be enjoyed, even the parts that hurt. All we need is for reality to take a backseat every once in awhile and just sit back and enjoy the ride.